THE Aftermath OF THE Wars against the Barbary Pirates

BRENDAN JANUARY

TFCB Twenty-First Century Books   MINNEAPOLIS

Consultant: James R. Arnold, military historian

The image on the jacket and the cover shows a fleet of Barbary pirates attacking a merchant ship in the 1600s (photo © Studio of Willem van de Velde II/The Bridgeman Art Library/Getty Images).

Twenty-First Century Books
A division of Lerner Publishing Group, Inc.
241 First Avenue North
Minneapolis, MN 55401 U.S.A.

Website address: www.lernerbooks.com

Library of Congress Cataloging-in-Publication Data

January, Brendan. 1972–
 The aftermath of the wars against the Barbary pirates / by Brendan January.
  p. cm. — (Aftermath of history)
 Includes bibliographical references and index.
 ISBN 978–0–8225–9094–1 (lib. bdg. : alk. paper)
 1. United States—History—Tripolitan War, 1801–1805—Juvenile literature. 2. United States—History—Tripolitan War, 1801–1805—Influence—Juvenile literature. I. Title.
 E335.J36 2009
 973.4'7—dc22   2008031021

Manufactured in the United States of America
1 2 3 4 5 6 — BP — 14 13 12 11 10 09

Contents

Pirates!

I N OCTOBER 1793, the U.S. representative in Lisbon, Portugal, heard disturbing news. Portugal had signed a treaty with Algiers, an African state on the coast of the Mediterranean Sea. For hundreds of years, Algerine pirates had captured foreign ships on the Mediterranean, seizing the ships and their cargoes for themselves and selling the sailors into slavery. To protect their merchant (trade) ships, European nations had long paid tribute to Algiers, paying it to leave European ships alone.

Portugal's navy normally patrolled the narrow Strait of Gibraltar separating Spain and Africa, and thereby bottling up the Algerines in the Mediterranean Sea. But the new treaty allowed the Algerines to sail out into the Atlantic Ocean. Soon a fleet of eight Algerine pirate ships was prowling the Atlantic sea-lanes.

In 1793 the United States was a young nation, and it paid no tribute to Algiers. The U.S. representative in Lisbon feared that Algerines were hunting for U.S. ships in the Atlantic. He warned, "Give a universal alarm to all citizens of the United States concerned in navigation, particularly to the southern parts of Europe, of the danger of being captured."

Algerine pirates sailed in small, swift craft, which caught the wind with their sails and were rowed in calm winds. The Algerines used their speed to pull alongside merchant ships. At a signal, the pirates would jump over a ship's rail and swarm over the deck, killing anyone who was brave—or foolish—enough to resist.

Edward Church, another U.S. official in Portugal, reported, "I have not slept since Receipt of the news of this hellish plot. Another corsair [pirate crew] in the Atlantic—God preserve us." Church was right to be terrified. In just two months, the Algerines captured eleven U.S. merchant ships and enslaved more than one hundred U.S. sailors.

"When they boarded us they even took the clothes from our backs," wrote David Pierce, a sailor captured from a schooner (two-masted ship) bound for Boston, Massachusetts. The pirates took Pierce and the other captives back to the city of Algiers. When they landed, continued Pierce, "we were all put into Chains and put to hard labor day and night with only the allowance of two black loaves [of bread] and water. Death would be a great relief and more welcome than a continuance of our present situation."

The men lived in one of the city's jails, crammed in with another six hundred prisoners. At three in the morning, guards woke the men, lined them up, and secured them to a giant metal chain. In addition, guards tethered each man to a 20- to 30-pound (9- to 14-kilogram) iron ball. When walking, each prisoner had to heft the ball along with him. Pierce described daily beatings: "Our driver carries a stick big enough to Knock a man down, and the innocent often suffer with the guilty." The guards tolerated no resistance. Simply talking back to them could earn a prisoner 150 to 200 bastinadoes, or the beating of the bare feet with a wooden rod.

The men worked all day, chipping stone from a mountain and then hauling it to the harbor, where they dumped the piles of rock into the water to create a landfill. The day ended a little before sunset, when the prisoners marched back to the jail.

The Algerine ruler—called the dey—allowed the Americans to write letters home. He hoped that people in the United States would offer money to free the captives, and the dey was always willing to release a prisoner for the right price. "We ask you in the name of your Father in heaven," wrote one U.S. sea captain, "to have compassion on our miseries. Lift up your voices like a trumpet; cry aloud in the cause of humanity."

In the United States, newspapers reprinted the prisoners' letters. In churches, local taverns, and the halls of Congress, citizens discussed the threat posed by Algiers. In response to the pirates, the United States began building a navy and became entangled in its first declared war with a foreign country. It also carried out its first covert, or secret, operation on foreign soil.

The conflict with the pirates—called the Barbary Wars—was the first "small war" in U.S. history. Unlike "large wars" such as World War I (1914–1918) and World War II (1939–1945), small wars are those that don't involve big armies facing off on battlefields. These wars, for the most part, do not receive major attention in U.S. history textbooks. They are often undeclared wars. But although small and little known, these wars can be just as long, bloody, and vicious as large wars.

In the aftermath of the Barbary Wars, the United States fought more small wars in the nineteenth and twentieth centuries. These wars had numerous purposes, such as protecting U.S. merchant ships and U.S. citizens or establishing and protecting the nation's overseas territories. Elite fighting units—often the U.S. Marines—did the bulk of the fighting. The United States never deployed its entire military force in these wars.

Although small, these wars have had an enormous impact on U.S. and world history. And the United States is still applying the lessons of these conflicts as it fights what is arguably the most important small war in its history: the War on Terror.

CHAPTER 1

Test for a New Nation

ALGIERS WAS ONE OF FOUR Barbary States along the coast of North Africa. The others were Tunis, Tripoli, and Morocco. For hundreds of years, the Barbary States were a part of the Ottoman Empire, based in modern-day Turkey. The empire was Islamic. Most of its people practiced Islam, a religion founded on the Arabian Peninsula in the A.D. 600s. The Ottomans, however, exercised little day-to-day power over the Barbary States.

The four Barbary States all sent pirates onto the Mediterranean Sea. The Barbary rulers considered the sea to be their ocean, and anyone who wished to sail it had to pay them for the privilege. Refusal to pay tribute was seen as an act of war. Barbary rulers felt justified in seizing the ships of nations that refused to pay.

The pirates had been active for centuries, sometimes even sailing outside the Mediterranean Sea to plunder. In the 1600s, Barbary pirates had roamed widely around the coasts of western Europe. In European harbors, pirate ships would suddenly appear. Carrying curved swords called scimitars, pirates would swoop out of their wooden vessels and seize as many goods and captives as they could.

In 1646, after Algerine pirates had seized hundreds of English citizens, the English Parliament, or legislature, decided to pay tribute to Algiers. This agreement soon evolved into formal treaties between England and all the Barbary States. In return for regular payments, the Barbary rulers agreed not to harass English merchant ships.

BARBAROSSA "RED BEARD" KHAYR AD-DIN WAS ONE OF THE MOST FAMOUS BARBARY PIRATES. HE LIVED IN THE 1500s, WHEN THE OTTOMAN EMPIRE RULED THE BARBARY STATES.

Other European nations followed England's example by signing treaties with the Barbary States, and representatives of European nations took up residence in Barbary capital cities. In addition to annual tribute, the European representatives distributed gifts and bribes to Barbary rulers, which helped keep the Mediterranean shipping lanes safe for European ships.

This was a practical policy. The Barbary States did not maintain

WILLEM VAN DE VELDE THE YOUNGER, A DUTCH PAINTER OF THE SEVENTEENTH CENTURY, PAINTED THIS SCENE OF BARBARY PIRATES ATTACKING SPANISH NAVAL SHIPS. THE PIRATES WOULD RAID EUROPEAN TRADING VESSELS IN SEARCH OF SLAVES AND TRADE GOODS. NATIONS THAT DID NOT PAY THE BARBARY STATES A TRIBUTE FOR SAFE PASSAGE RISKED ATTACK BY PIRATES.

powerful navies as the big European countries did. But France, England, and other strong European states were too busy fighting wars with one another to divert attention and resources to the Barbary States. Instead, they simply paid tribute.

Many of the smaller, poorer nations of Europe couldn't pay the Barbary rulers, however, and Barbary pirates often captured their sailors. In the capitals of the Barbary Coast nations, slave auctions were common. Most of the European slaves were Christian, whereas their enslavers were Muslim (followers of Islam). "Christians are cheap today" was a well-worn joke, told whenever a ship with slaves arrived in a Barbary port.

A New Nation Confronts Piracy

In 1783, after several years of war, the thirteen colonies along the east coast of North America won independence from Great Britain. The colonies became a separate country, the United States of America.

Americans were overjoyed at winning independence, but the young country found itself alone in a very hostile world. When they had been a part of the British Empire, North American colonists had enjoyed the protection of the mighty British fleet. American merchant ships, flying the British flag, had safe access to virtually any port in the world. With independence, however, this protection vanished.

Shipping was critically important to the new U.S. economy. As Americans pushed west to clear land, lay roads, and build towns, they

Before the U.S. Navy

DURING THE AMERICAN REVOLUTION (1775–1783), Americans outfitted some existing merchant ships with guns and also built some new warships. This makeshift navy never seriously challenged British naval supremacy. When British troops captured Philadelphia in 1777, they destroyed some new American ships under construction. The Americans had only one bright spot in the naval war with Britain. In 1779 commander John Paul Jones captured a British frigate (a light, midsized ship) after a savage battle in the Atlantic Ocean.

also ventured onto the sea. The majority of Americans at the time lived close to the Atlantic Ocean, and all big U.S. cities—Boston, New York, Philadelphia, and Charleston—were ports. Ships carried crops, timber, and other raw materials from North America across the Atlantic Ocean to markets in Europe. In turn, ships carried manufactured goods and settlers from Europe to the United States, as well as slaves from Africa.

The British, smarting from their defeat in the American Revolution, were determined to crush U.S. competition with their own merchant ships. Great Britain prohibited U.S. ships from trading in the British West Indies, a group of islands in the eastern Caribbean Sea. Blocked from this region, the Americans sought other markets, including those in southern Europe on the Mediterranean coast. In the mid-1780s, more than one hundred U.S. merchant ships sailed into the Mediterranean each year.

Inevitably some of these ships fell prey to pirates. In 1784 Algerines captured the U.S. schooner *Maria*. The pirates stripped the six U.S. crewmen of everything they owned, including their clothes, and stowed the crew in the filthy hold of the pirate ship, which was already jammed with more than thirty captives from other ships. In Algiers the pirates gave the prisoners clothing and marched them through the streets in front of jeering crowds. After three days in a prison, the captives were auctioned at the city's slave market.

Then Barbary pirates seized another U.S. ship. Rumors spread in the United States that statesman Benjamin Franklin had fallen into pirates' hands while sailing home from France. The account was false, and Franklin arrived in the United States safely. But like most spectacular stories, this one spread quickly, fixing U.S. attention on the Barbary pirates.

U.S. officials contacted the Barbary States and tried to negotiate. Thomas Jefferson and John Adams were U.S. ambassadors in Europe at the time. They contacted the ambassador of Tripoli for an explanation. Why did the Tripolitans commit acts of piracy? "The Ambassador answered us that it was founded on the laws of the Prophet [Muhammad, the founder of Islam]," Jefferson later wrote, "that it was written in their Koran [or Quran, the holy book of Islam], that all nations who should not have acknowledged [Muslim] authority were sinners, that it was their right and duty to make war upon them wherever they could be found, and to make slaves of all they could take as Prisoners."

Although both Jefferson and Adams despised the idea of paying bribes, Adams noted that paying tribute would probably be cheaper than going to war. The United States depended heavily on shipping its goods to Europe, and the threat from the Barbary States was a serious one. Adams advised Jefferson that the United States should not fight the Barbary States "unless we determine to fight them forever."

THE DEBATE OVER A NAVY

In 1790 Jefferson became the nation's first secretary of state. In this position, he was responsible for U.S. relations with other nations. Jefferson listed three options for dealing with the Barbary States: pay tribute each year, pay ransom when Americans were captured, or fight.

Jefferson preferred to fight. He believed that paying ransoms for captives would simply encourage the Barbary States to take more prisoners and to raise the price for each hostage. Jefferson found annual tribute shameful. The Barbary pirates, in his view, were little more than thieves.

EARLY U.S. LEADERS, INCLUDING PRESIDENT GEORGE WASHINGTON *(RIGHT)*, SECRETARY OF STATE THOMAS JEFFERSON *(SEATED LEFT)*, AND SECRETARY OF THE TREASURY ALEXANDER HAMILTON *(CENTER)*, HAD TO DECIDE HOW TO HANDLE THE PIRACY THEIR SHIPS FACED IN THE MEDITERRANEAN SEA. WOULD THEY PAY TRIBUTE? OR WOULD THEY CHOOSE FORCE?

Moreover, argued Jefferson, the pirates weren't very power-ful—despite their fierce reputation. While in Paris, France, as U.S. ambassador, Jefferson had closely questioned friends and officials about the Barbary pirates. He had learned that none of the Barbary States maintained a real navy. Instead, they had pirates cruise the Mediterranean in swift but small craft. These boats could not sustain cannon fire from big ships.

Jefferson recommended that the United States send naval ships to patrol the waters outside Barbary ports. None of the pirate ships would challenge large naval ships and thus would be trapped in their harbors. Protected by this blockade, U.S merchant ships would be able to sail the Mediterranean without fear.

The U.S. Congress reacted enthusiastically to Jefferson's proposal but also regarded it as too expensive. The young nation was still struggling to balance its budget, and the government had few sources of new revenue.

Then, in 1793, came news of the Algerine seizure of more U.S. merchant ships. The enslaved captain's plea to Americans "to have compassion on our miseries" evoked sympathy in the United States. Moreover, piracy made U.S. shipping difficult, dangerous, and expensive, creating tough economic times in the United States. Sailors refused to join ships bound for the Mediterranean, regardless of pay.

This turmoil—and the lurid, grim stories of the captures—circulated through U.S. newspapers. Congress had to do something and once again faced the question of whether they should pay tribute or fight. The mood in the country favored force, but Congress had to grapple with the problem of building and then paying for the naval power needed to attack the pirates.

The decision was about far more than just the Barbary pirates. The young United States was defining its national identity. The newspapers urged war, and people in the streets shouted support for it. Everyone knew that war meant violence and death. For the victors, it also meant pride and glory. But the true consequences of war extended much further.

To wage war, the nation would have to support an army or a navy or both. Building an army and a navy meant training officers, equipping soldiers, and gathering supplies. A navy also required ships. Once built, ships needed repair and maintenance.

All of this cost money—and lots of it. War is, above all, expensive. To build a military and wage war, the government would have to tax people more heavily to get the needed funds. Taxation was an important issue to Americans. They had fought the American Revolution largely because they believed the British government had taxed them unfairly.

In addition, taxes are the food that feeds government and allows it to grow. A government that grows large, some argued, would be more likely to seize power from individual citizens. Many in Congress opposed creating an army and navy because they would lead to higher taxes and a larger government that might destroy U.S. liberties. They believed that a war abroad would lead to a loss of freedom at home.

William Maclay, a senator from Pennsylvania, attacked the idea of a navy. He described it as a plot to raise taxes. When tax collectors spread out through the land, "farewell freedom in America," he said. Maclay also decried a loss of U.S. innocence. Building a navy, he wrote, would make the United States warlike, "like all other nations." He regarded building a military as setting "aside a portion of our citizens for the purpose of inflicting misery on our fellow mortals."

On the other side of the debate, many voices brought up notions of honor and justice. It was a dangerous world, and the United States had to establish a strong image, the pro-war factions argued. The European powers were seeking to "clip the wings by which we may soar to dangerous greatness," wrote one supporter. Another claimed that "our flag is about as much respected among the different nations as an old rag that's hung up in a cornfield to scare crows." The United States could not afford a reputation as a weak nation that could not protect its interests, some said. The Barbary pirates offered a chance to show the world that the United States would not be bullied.

> *"[The American] flag is about as much respected among the different nations as an old rag that's hung up in a cornfield to scare crows."*
> —a supporter of increasing U.S. military power, 1793

Other war advocates brought up the importance of trade to the nation's economy. "If we mean to have commerce," wrote one supporter, "then we must have a naval force to defend it."

Ultimately, the supporters of building a navy won out. After four months of argument and counterargument, Congress passed a bill providing $688,888 to construct and equip six warships. On March 27, 1794, President George Washington signed the bill into law. Americans remember that date as the birthday of the U.S. Navy.

BUILDING THE U.S. NAVY

To supervise construction of the navy, President Washington turned to an old and trusted friend, Henry Knox. This genial former bookstore owner had served as an officer in the American Revolution, where he had established a reputation for getting things done. When Washington became president, he appointed Knox as secretary of war. The passage of the navy bill gave Knox great responsibility.

Knox was fortunate that the nation's capital then was in Philadelphia, Pennsylvania. Philadelphia, on the banks of the Delaware River, was the largest city and port in North America. Its riverfront was crowded with storehouses and the masts of ships. Shipyards stretched north and south along the riverbank. On any given day, hundreds of craftspeople, supervisors, and ship designers swarmed over the giant wooden frames of new ships—hammering, sawing, and smearing hot, black pitch over the hulls to waterproof them. Though Knox himself knew little about shipbuilding, he could draw on an enormous pool of talent, skill, and experience in Philadelphia.

A Novel Design

Knox found a designer in Joshua Humphreys, who had built and repaired more than three hundred merchant ships over a nearly thirty-year career. Most navies at the time were dominated by two types of ships: massive "ships of the line" that carried fifty to one hundred guns and smaller (but still large) frigates with twenty-four to fifty guns. The ships of the line (so called because they sailed into battle in a line) carried enormous firepower but were slow and cumbersome compared to the smaller, faster frigates. For the new U.S. fleet, Humphreys sought to combine the best features of both ships. He designed huge frigates that carried more guns than normal: forty-four. These frigates would have the advantage in fights with ordinary frigates. They were also built for speed, so they could outrun heavier battleships and escape an unequal contest.

SHIPBUILDERS IN PHILADELPHIA BUILD A FRIGATE PLANK BY PLANK IN 1800. THIS ENGRAVING WAS MADE BY WILLIAM RUSSELL BIRCH AND THOMAS BIRCH THAT SAME YEAR.

Humphreys insisted that shipbuilders execute his designs perfectly from the best materials. He ordered the decks cut from Carolina pine trees and the planks fashioned from red cedar. The structure of the ship—the skeleton that held it together—was to come from southern live oak, a massive tree with tough, durable, and heavy wood. This tree grew in only one place on the planet: along the coast of the southern United States.

Humphreys sent work crews to cut enough wood from southern live oak trees for all six ships. The crews established camps on uninhabited islands off the coast of Georgia. Battling heat, rain, and mosquitoes, they felled the oak trees, cut up big pieces of wood, and shipped the wood north.

War at Sea

WHEN AN EIGHTEENTH-CENTURY NAVAL ship entered battle, each sailor had a different task. A boy called a powder monkey was in charge of toting bags of gunpowder from deep in the ship's hold.

Teams of sailors operated each of the ship's guns. In preparation for firing, they opened the gun ports and removed the stoppers that kept seawater out of the guns' muzzles. When the powder monkey arrived, one sailor would grab the powder and push it down the gun barrel with a rammer. Another would put a cannonball (or smaller pieces of metal designed to scatter upon firing) into the gun barrel. After loading the gun, the crew pushed its snout through the open gun port. The crew captain sprinkled more gunpowder into a shallow hole at the butt of the cannon. Another sailor lit a fuse.

The gun crews were trained to fire together in a broadside—coordinated shots from all the guns on one side of the ship. With a thunderous roar, a broadside hurled metal at the opposing ship. Cannonballs and metal pieces smashed into the enemy ship's hull, clipped the rigging, and shredded the sails.

The most devastating impact was on men. It was not uncommon for a veteran naval officer or sailor of this era to be missing a limb—torn off by an enemy cannonball. Following the sudden silence after a broadside, screams could usually be heard across the water.

Each ship tried to gain an advantage, turning this way and that so that a broadside would do the most damage, while also avoiding the opponent's guns. It was an intricate and deadly ballet. At the climax of a naval battle, ships sometimes drew close enough for one crew to board the enemy ship. In this situation, the battle often descended into a wild scramble of slashing swords, roaring muskets, and pistol fire.

Every U.S. naval ship carried a small group of men specially trained for such close encounters: marines. The marines carried muskets and stood on platforms on the ship's masts. Perched high above the decks, they had a clear shot at the enemy.

It took six months for the first shipment of wood to arrive in Philadelphia. Under Humphreys' critical eye, the shipyard began assembling the giant pieces. Humphreys was disgusted with the second shipment of wood, which he said was not of high enough quality. After work resumed, a series of additional delays dragged out the timetable for completion.

Negotiating

In the meantime, Dey Hassan Pasha, the ruler of Algiers, had heard of the construction of the U.S. frigates. He sent a message to U.S. leaders, suggesting that for $2.5 million and two frigates, he might release 119 U.S. prisoners and make peace with the United States. The Americans were dismayed. This was a staggering price that would consume a major portion of the U.S. government's annual budget. Although Thomas Jefferson bristled at the idea of paying tribute, other U.S. leaders were eager for peace with Algiers. The Americans agreed to negotiate.

When U.S. representative Joseph Donaldson arrived in Algiers, he offered $500,000 instead of $2.5 million. Richard O'Brien, a prisoner who had become the dey's clerk and the spokesperson for the other U.S. prisoners, aided Donaldson in the negotiations.

The negotiations went back and forth. The dey finally settled for $642,000, along with $21,400 per year in weapons and ammunition. On September 5, 1795, the treaty was settled, and a twenty-one-gun salute echoed over the Algiers harbor. The U.S. prisoners, some of them captives for more than ten years, rejoiced.

Then they had to wait, because the Americans needed several months to secure the money. Because of the delay, the Americans promised to deliver a ship to the dey as a gift. The craft was a light frigate called the *Crescent* designed by Humphreys, the same man who was overseeing construction of the U.S. Navy.

The terms of the treaty humiliated the United States. The payment was high, and the *Crescent* would soon threaten other ships in the Mediterranean. However, the United States thought the deal was worth it. Algiers was the most powerful of the Barbary States. By making peace with the dey, the United States was also able to sign treaties with Tunis and Tripoli. These treaties included small amounts of tribute—about $56,000 for Tripoli and $107,000 for Tunis. After the Senate ratified these treaties, U.S. ships could safely sail the Mediterranean Sea.

CHAPTER 2

War on the Barbary Coast

IN 1797 PRESIDENT GEORGE WASHINGTON left office, and John Adams replaced him. Among his first decisions, Adams sent three U.S. ambassadors to the Barbary States. Richard O'Brien, by then freed from captivity, returned to Algiers as the U.S. ambassador. James Cathcart, who had also been a prisoner in Algiers, would go to Tripoli. William Eaton, a former captain in the U.S. Army, would travel to Tunis.

Eaton had fought in the American Revolution and in clashes with Native Americans on the western frontier. He had long nurtured a fascination with Africa and the Middle East. He read the Quran and had studied a book on the Ottoman Empire. He wrote in his diary, "I wish to learn Arabic [the language of the Muslim rulers] and to find out all I can about the Ottomans. Some day I shall visit that far-off part of the world, and if the almighty wishes it for me, may even live there for a time. Therefore all I can discover and learn will be of use to me later." The appointment to Tunis fulfilled this wish.

In 1798 the three U.S. ambassadors arrived in Algiers. Within two days, Eaton and Cathcart gained an audience with the Algerine dey. The dey's bodyguards searched the men and took their swords and then ushered them into the dey's throne room. Eaton described the dey as a "huge shaggy beast, sitting on his rump upon a low bench covered with a cushion of embroidered velvet, with his hind legs gathered up like a tailor, or a bear. On our approach to him, he reached out his forepaw as if to receive something to eat. Our guide exclaimed 'Kiss the Dey's hand!'"

WILLIAM EATON HAD SERVED IN GEORGE WASHINGTON'S CONTINENTAL ARMY (1780–1783). HE WAS NAMED A CONSUL TO TUNIS IN 1797.

WAR

Eaton moved on to Tunis, and Cathcart went to his post in Tripoli. Tripoli was an ancient city. An arch in honor of the Roman emperor—built more than fifteen hundred years before, when Tripoli was part of the Roman Empire—still stood in a vegetable market. When Cathcart arrived, the city consisted of low, whitewashed buildings with flat roofs. Thick walls surrounded the three sides of the city facing land. A stone castle studded with black cannons defended the city.

The leader of Tripoli, called the pasha, was Yusuf Qaramanli. He lived within the stone castle in luxury. His throne room had a marble floor and porcelain walls. His mosaic-covered throne rose 4 feet (1.2 meters) high. Its fringed velvet cushion flashed with brilliant jewels. The pasha also wore flashy clothing: a silk robe covered with shimmering tinsel and gold, a diamond-studded belt, and a white turban decorated with ribbons. A dark beard flowed over his chest. The pasha looked like someone who was used to giving orders—and having them obeyed.

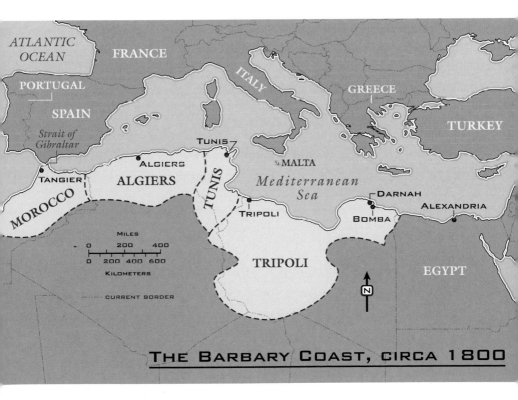

THE BARBARY COAST, CIRCA 1800

Qaramanli soon told Cathcart that he was dissatisfied with Tripoli's treaty with the United States. He had seen other Barbary States receive more money from the United States, and he wanted what he regarded as his fair share. He demanded a $225,000 cash payment and $25,000 per year. He gave the Americans six months to accept his terms.

In October 1800, Cathcart wrote to leaders in Washington, D.C., the new U.S. capital, about Qaramanli's demands. At a time when most ships sailed at the speed of a walking person, it would take months for the message to arrive. But the delay mattered little, because Qaramanli had no real intention of negotiating.

A New President Faces an Old Problem

As Cathcart's letters made their way slowly across the ocean, a new administration was taking power in Washington, D.C. Thomas Jefferson, the newly elected president, took the oath of office in March 1801. Jefferson barely had time to get used to the White House before he learned of the latest crisis with the Barbary States. He had become very familiar with the problem, first as a diplomat in Europe and then as secretary of state under George Washington. Throughout his career, Jefferson had advocated force to deal with the pirates. In a letter to a friend, Jefferson had written that he was an "enemy" of paying bribes to the Barbary pirates. "I know that nothing will stop the eternal increase [requests for increased tribute] from these pirates but the presence of an armed force."

As Jefferson pondered his options, tensions increased in Tripoli. On May 14, 1801, Yusuf Qaramanli's soldiers marched to the U.S.

consulate and chopped down the flagpole. The act represented a declaration of war against the United States. James Cathcart, fearing capture, left the country.

Jefferson called his cabinet (council of advisers) to the White House. He said that he wanted to send a naval force to the Mediterranean Sea to show the Barbary States that the United States could fight if necessary. The cabinet debated. No one wanted to pay more tribute to the Barbary pirates, but Jefferson's proposal would send U.S. sailors around the world and potentially into harm's way. U.S. ships might have to fire upon ships from another country, leading to war. The cabinet also considered an important question: Only Congress had the authority to declare war, but could the president make a warlike decision without Congress?

Jefferson ordered a U.S. squadron to set sail. He acted without congressional approval in part because Congress was not in session. The members of the House of Representatives and the Senate were scattered throughout the states. Even if Jefferson had called them together for a special meeting, in this age of stagecoach and horse travel, it would have taken weeks for them to make the trip. Because the situation was an emergency, Jefferson believed that he, as president of the United States, was justified to act on his own.

A DEMONSTRATION OF FORCE

The U.S. squadron left Virginia on June 2. It was a formidable force, led by Commodore Richard Dale in the brand-new frigate USS *President*. The rest of the force consisted of two more frigates, *Philadelphia* and *Essex*, as well as a smaller sloop, *Enterprise*. Together, the fleet carried more than one hundred heavy guns. In the warm June

THIS PAINTING FROM AROUND 1800 SHOWS THE USS *PRESIDENT* HEADING OUT ACROSS CHOPPY WATERS.

weather, the ships' sails billowed and filled with wind, pulling the fleet east.

Although the sailors on the ships were unaware that Tripoli had declared war against the United States, they expected it soon anyway. As the ships made their way across the ocean, the sailors drilled repeatedly on the ships' guns. After several weeks, the squadron arrived off the coast of Tripoli and imposed a blockade, preventing large Tripolitan ships from leaving the harbor.

By late July, drinking water on the ships was running low. Dale ordered the commander of the *Enterprise*, Andrew Sterrett, to sail to the island of Malta to refill. As Sterrett made his way to Malta, he spotted a ship on the horizon. It appeared to be a Barbary pirate ship. Sterrett immediately ordered his crew to prepare for action, calling the sailors to the ship's twelve guns. This was a moment they had spent months training for.

The *Enterprise* was flying a British flag as it approached the

Heavy Guns

IN THE EARLY NINETEENTH century, a ship's firepower was measured by the weight of its cannonballs. A 24-pound (10 kg) gun fired 24-pound cannonballs, a 12-pound (5 kg) gun fired 12-pound cannonballs, and so on. Thus a broadside from ten 24-pound guns fired 240 pounds (109 kg) of iron into an enemy ship. Although ship commanders liked to draw close before firing their guns, a 24-pound gun could also do damage at long range. The cannon could fire a ball more than 1,000 yards (914 m).

Barbary ship. Flying a false flag was a common part of the cat-and-mouse game that made up naval warfare at that time. Identifying your enemies before they correctly identified you could make the difference between escaping or being sunk or captured. All sailing ships kept a number of flags from different nations for just this purpose.

The captain of the Barbary ship, the *Tripoli*, never imagined that he would meet a U.S. warship in the Mediterranean. The two ships drew close enough for the men on board to speak. Sterrett called out, asking the ship to identify itself and explain what it was doing. The *Tripoli*'s captain, Ra'is Muhammad Rous, answered that he was searching for U.S. merchant ships to capture.

This was the worst answer Rous could have given. Sterrett immediately ordered the British flag lowered and the U.S. flag raised. *Enterprise* sent several broadsides crashing into *Tripoli*. *Tripoli*'s gunners were not as well trained as the Americans. Their cannons fired at different times and with poor aim.

Outgunned, Rous tried to steer his ship close to *Enterprise* so that his sailors could board it. At this point, marines aboard *Enterprise* fired their muskets at the men gathered on *Tripoli*'s deck. Several fell, and the two ships drew apart.

Enterprise continued to fire, shattering *Tripoli*. Rous ordered his ship's colors, or flag, lowered—a signal of surrender. The sailors aboard *Enterprise* cheered. But as *Enterprise* drew near to seize the ship, Rous had the colors raised again. His sailors again tried to board *Enterprise*. Sterrett quickly steered clear and fired another broadside into *Tripoli*, while the marines shot down more pirates on the deck.

Rous again ordered the colors lowered. This time, however, Sterrett ordered his gunners to keep firing, pounding *Tripoli* into a wreck. Of its eighty-man crew, thirty were killed and thirty wounded. Realizing that the Americans would not stop firing just because his flag was lowered, Rous finally hurled it into the sea. This time his surrender was honest. The Americans stopped firing and boarded the stricken

THIS DRAWING, CREATED AFTER AN 1878 ARWORK BY WILLIAM BAINBRIDGE HOFF, SHOWS THE USS *ENTERPRISE* CAPTURING THE *TRIPOLI* IN 1801. THE UNITED STATES WANTED TO SEND A MESSAGE TO THE PIRATES OF THE BARBARY COAST AND OTHER ENEMIES ABROAD THAT IT WAS GOING TO DEFEND ITSELF AROUND THE WORLD.

vessel. Not one U.S. sailor had been wounded in the exchange—testament to Sterrett's skill and his sailors' training.

Sterrett, uncertain whether the United States had formally declared war on *Tripoli*, did not take *Tripoli* as a prize. Instead, he threw the ship's guns overboard and allowed Tripoli to rig a new sail and limp home. When the ship arrived in Tripoli, Yusuf Qaramanli was outraged at the defeat. He had Rous mounted backward on a donkey, with sheep intestines strewn around his neck, and paraded through the city's streets. As if that humiliation wasn't enough, Qaramanli ordered the unfortunate admiral an additional punishment: five hundred bastinadoes.

EVERYTHING SHORT OF WAR

Despite the fighting, Qaramanli's hostility, and Jefferson's urging, the U.S. Congress would not declare war on Tripoli—partly because war was still a painful memory for many congressmen who had lived through the American Revolution, and they were not ready to go to war again. However, in early 1802, Congress passed a bill that allowed U.S. naval ships to attack and seize Tripolitan vessels. In addition, Congress gave President Jefferson greater authority to send ships and sailors to Tripoli. Congress would not declare war, but it essentially gave Jefferson and the U.S. Navy the means to wage it.

Jefferson moved quickly to bolster the U.S. presence in the Mediterranean. He appointed a new commander of the fleet, Commodore Richard Morris, and gave him five more ships—all frigates. With this force, Jefferson expected Morris to quickly defeat the Barbary pirates.

Like Dale before him, Commodore Morris had orders to blockade Tripoli, preventing merchant ships or pirates from leaving the city.

But Morris believed that a blockade would not be effective. Instead, he ordered the frigates to sail with U.S. merchant ships together in convoys, or large groups. The frigates would protect the merchant ships from attack.

Without a blockade, there were no encounters between U.S. ships and Tripolitan ships. This lack of confrontation drew contempt from Tripoli and frustrated rage from officers serving under Morris. Worse, Morris had arrived in the Mediterranean with his wife and son, drawing sarcastic commentary throughout the fleet. William Eaton fumed, "Who . . . would ever bring a wife to war against the ferocious savages of Barbary?"

Infuriated and discouraged, Jefferson replaced Morris with Edward Preble. A proven fighter, Preble had joined a privateer (an armed private ship used in wartime) at the age of sixteen, during the American Revolution. Constantly irritated by painful stomach ulcers, he was known for his short temper and exacting standards. But Jefferson realized that force might not be enough, so he appointed Tobias Lear, formerly George Washington's personal secretary, to negotiate peace with Tripoli if the navy could not force Qaramanli to surrender.

Eaton Schemes

As Preble took command of the U.S. fleet, William Eaton remained in Tunis. He disliked his work at the Tunisian court, where he was supposed to dole out gifts to the Tunisian ruler. He was incensed that U.S. money was being dispersed to buy "oil of roses to perfume a pirate's beard!" He went on to ask, "Why this humiliation? Why furnish them the means to cut our own throats?"

Acting on his own, Eaton devised various plots and schemes to

> *"I can guarantee the president and the Congress
> that the rulers of the Barbary coast will sing a
> new song, more to our liking."*
>
> —William Eaton, 1802

conquer Tripoli—some realistic and some absurd. He wrote to Secretary of State James Madison, asking for troops and ships. With a navy and army, he wrote, "I can guarantee the president and the Congress that the rulers of the Barbary coast will sing a new song, more to our liking."

Then Eaton met Ahmad Qaramanli, the older brother of Yusuf. From Ahmad, Eaton learned that the Qaramanli family history was soaked with blood. At the age of twenty, Yusuf had murdered his eldest brother, Hassan, in front of their mother. Yusuf had then fought against Ahmad for control of Tripoli. After many twists and turns, Ahmad took the throne in 1795.

Ahmad was an agreeable but weak ruler, whose first reaction to at least one crisis was to faint. His reign was predictably short. Yusuf literally locked Ahmad out of Tripoli and proclaimed himself the new pasha. Ahmad ultimately fled to Tunis to escape his brother, while Yusuf seized Ahmad's wife and five children and held them in his castle as hostages.

Eaton believed Ahmad was the ideal weapon in the war against Yusuf. He devised a plan: He and Ahmad would mount an expedition to topple Yusuf and put Ahmad back on the throne. Ahmad would sign a treaty permanently releasing the United States from paying tribute to Tripoli, and Ahmad would pay for the whole operation (estimated to cost about ten thousand dollars) once he became ruler of Tripoli.

Returning to the United States, Eaton circulated his plan among top officials in Washington. Ahmad also wrote a letter to President Jefferson, claiming that if the U.S. Navy supported him, he would march on Tripoli with "a hundred thousand men." Jefferson, however, was not ready to approve the operation.

THE CAPTURE OF THE *PHILADELPHIA*

Meanwhile, the conflict with Tripoli heated up. On October 31, 1803, the thirty-eight-gun frigate *Philadelphia*, commanded by William Bainbridge, was on patrol outside Tripoli. Early that morning, *Philadelphia*'s lookout spotted a small Tripolitan ship racing toward the harbor.

Bainbridge ordered his ship to chase. Over two hours, the larger frigate gained on the smaller craft—but then neared the Tripoli harbor. This was dangerous water, where ridges of sand rose up rapidly from the seabed, making a treacherous underwater mountain range that only local guides knew how to navigate.

Philadelphia suddenly struck rock and sand and shuddered to a halt. The bow of the ship had ridden up onto a sandbar, leaving the stern deeper in the water. Within sight of the Tripoli harbor, *Philadelphia* was stuck. Bainbridge tried to catch the wind and drive the ship over the reef. This effort only drove the ship farther onto the sandbar. He then ordered sailors to heave most of the ship's cannons over the side. Bainbridge hoped to make the ship light enough to float free. This effort failed too.

There was movement in the Tripoli harbor. Seeing that the frigate had run aground, Tripolitan pirate ships began to emerge. Within a

An engraving based on a drawing by Charles Denoon shows the *Philadelphia* surrounded by Tripolitan gunboats after it became stranded on a sandbar in the Tripoli harbor in October 1803. The ship could neither break loose into open waters nor defend itself from the heavy fire.

few hours, about ten small ships surrounded *Philadelphia*. By this time, the frigate was leaning on its side and the crew had pitched most of the weapons overboard. The giant ship was defenseless.

Bainbridge ordered the flag lowered as a sign of surrender. With whoops and yells of victory, pirates swarmed over the craft, stripping the crew of their clothing and taking everything of value from below deck. The 307 men of the *Philadelphia* were prisoners.

A Daring Operation

Yusuf Qaramanli renamed *Philadelphia* the *Gift of Allah*. (Allah is the Arabic word for God.) Qaramanli planned to make it a pirate ship. He was thrilled with the idea of a former U.S. naval ship roaming the Mediterranean and capturing merchant ships. Commodore Preble, however, devised a plot with his lieutenant, Stephen Decatur, to destroy *Philadelphia* in the Tripoli harbor. They were determined not to let Qaramanli use an American ship for piracy.

Preble and Decatur planned to conceal a raiding party of Americans within a small ship and sail into the Tripoli harbor at night. The Americans would pull alongside *Philadelphia*, board it, overwhelm its Tripolitan crew, and set the ship aflame.

The plan was daring and risky. If Tripolitans stopped the ship and uncovered the Americans before they could reach *Philadelphia*, there was little chance that Decatur or any of his crew would escape. The harbor was crowded with the pasha's ships, and the castle's battery of heavy guns could sink any vessel in the harbor. To enter the harbor, navigate through its reefs, and surprise *Philadelphia*, the Americans would have to do their work silently and quickly. They would use bladed instruments—swords, daggers, and hatchets.

On the night of February 16, the U.S. craft—called *Intrepid*—slipped into the harbor and approached *Philadelphia*. To disguise their nationality, the Americans on deck wore the clothing of ordinary European seamen. Below deck, Decatur and sixty more Americans waited.

As the small vessel coasted silently toward *Philadelphia*, its Tripolitan guards pointed their cannons as if to fire. On board *Intrepid*, a sailor who knew a smattering of Arabic asked the guards if he could tie up to *Philadelphia*. The sailor explained that his ship had lost its anchor in a recent storm. The Tripolitan guards relaxed. This kind of request was not unusual. *Intrepid* pulled up next to the larger ship and touched it. Then Decatur shouted, "Board!"

"The effect was truly electric," wrote one of the Americans. "Not

IN 1804 STEPHEN DECATUR LED HIS MEN IN A NIGHTTIME RAID
AGAINST THE TRIPOLITANS ABOARD THE USS *PHILADELPHIA*. THE
PLOT WORKED, AND THE AMERICANS DISABLED THE SHIP.

a man had been seen or heard to breathe a moment before; at the
next the boarders hung on the ship's side like a cluster of bees; and,
in another instant, every man was aboard the frigate." The Americans
attacked the guards and cut them down furiously. "Poor fellows!" a
U.S. sailor wrote later. "About 20 of them were cut to pieces and the
rest jumped overboard."

The Americans had achieved surprise, but the screams and whoops
of the hand-to-hand fighting echoed over the still harbor. Within minutes, two nearby ships began peppering *Philadelphia* with musket fire.
Americans on *Intrepid* passed boxes of flammable material—powder,

wood shavings, tar, and lint—through *Philadelphia*'s gun ports. Men carrying lanterns scrambled through the ship, scattering the material and setting it aflame.

Within fifteen minutes, the fires had spread through the ship and belched above the harbor. The Americans jumped back into *Intrepid*. Oarsmen pulled frantically, rowing *Intrepid* out of the harbor. Two hours later, they had escaped. On the horizon, *Philadelphia* burned like a torch—a "column of fire truly magnificent," recalled one of the Americans. Decatur had not lost a single man in the operation.

HOME FRONT

Word of the *Philadelphia* incident reached the United States in March 1804. Although the burning of the captured ship was heartening to Americans, *Philadelphia*'s crew remained captive. U.S. newspapers were filled with rage against Tripoli. One headline captured the mood: "Millions for Defense, but Not a Cent For Tribute!"

President Jefferson called on Congress to increase military spending, and Congress agreed to raise taxes to support the delivery of another naval squadron to the Mediterranean. In this atmosphere, William Eaton's plan found a more welcome audience. Jefferson authorized Eaton to return to the Mediterranean, find Ahmad

Qaramanli, overthrow Yusuf, and install Ahmad on the throne of Tripoli. President Jefferson promised to furnish Eaton with field artillery, one thousand muskets, and forty thousand dollars. He also gave Eaton a special title: navy agent of the United States for the several Barbary regencies.

Jefferson was the first president in U.S. history to authorize a covert operation to destabilize a foreign government. This was an extraordinary act. After all, Congress had not officially declared war on Tripoli. But Jefferson believed the operation was justified to protect U.S. interests.

Nonetheless, the operation made him uncomfortable. The United States was a new nation. Jefferson and other U.S. leaders believed that their country and government should be a model for the rest of the world. In their minds, a model country didn't meddle in the affairs of other nations. It seemed dishonorable.

A statement written by James Madison, Jefferson's secretary of state and close friend, reflected this unease. Madison wrote that the United States normally disapproved of interfering with another country's internal affairs. However, Madison continued, the United States was engaged in a "just war" with Tripoli. In such times, "it cannot be unfair" to use tactics such as covert operations.

CHAPTER 3

To the Shores of Tripoli

I N SUMMER 1804, William Eaton sailed with a U.S. fleet back to the Mediterranean. His mission had begun at last. A few months later, in mid-September, Commodore Preble agreed to give Eaton use of a ship, *Argus*, captained by thirty-one-year-old Isaac Hull. Preble ordered Hull to carry Eaton to Alexandria, Egypt, an ancient port city east of the Barbary States. Ahmad Qaramanli was reportedly somewhere in Egypt.

After weeks of frustrating delays, *Argus* arrived in Alexandria on November 25. Eaton then spent several weeks searching for Ahmad in lawless and war-torn Egypt, finally finding him in southern Egypt. The two men reunited outside Alexandria. There, Eaton settled on a plan to attack Tripoli. He decided to march an army more than 500 miles (804 kilometers) across northern Africa and attack Darnah, a city on the Tripolitan coast. From Darnah, Eaton's force would go on to fight Yusuf's army and then place Ahmad on the throne of Tripoli. The victory would also free the *Philadelphia* captives.

Hull prepared to depart Alexandria in *Argus*. Before he left, he loaned Eaton a handful of men—eight marines and a sailor. The marines included Lieutenant Presley Neville O'Bannon, a twenty-nine-year-old officer from Virginia. He was tough and brave and already strongly impressed by Eaton. "If [Eaton] wants us to march to hell . . . . we'll gladly go there," O'Bannon said. To support the few U.S. troops, Eaton hired a motley group that formed the core of his force. It included thirty-eight Greek soldiers as well as twenty-five other Europeans from a variety of nations.

In addition to this group, Ahmad Qaramanli had secured the loyalty of about two hundred Arab cavalry, or horsemen, and about ninety Arab followers. The Arabs were local Egyptians who practiced Islam. With a total force numbering a little more than four hundred, William Eaton and Ahmad Qaramanli joined up outside Alexandria.

The Arab World

WILLIAM EATON AND AHMAD Qaramanli's army was mostly made up of Arab Muslims from Egypt. Arabs are the dominant ethnic group in the Middle East. The first Arab people lived on the Arabian Peninsula, in modern-day Saudi Arabia. In the seventh century, most Arabs converted to Islam, a religion founded on the Arabian Peninsula in the 600s by the prophet Muhammad. Under a number of different rulers, Arabs conquered much of the Middle East as well as parts of Asia and Africa. The Arabs spread their language (Arabic), the Islamic religion, and Arab culture throughout the conquered territories. In modern times, political scientists use the term *Arab world* to refer to eighteen countries in the Middle East and North Africa.

For the upcoming journey, the force had twenty-five bags of rice, eighteen barrels of biscuits, sixty-eight bags of beans, and ninety bags of barley. For drinking, the force carried fourteen bottles of brandy and two casks of wine, each holding 63 gallons (238 liters). More critically, the men would rely on wells and water holes along the way for fresh drinking water. To carry the supplies, Eaton haggled with local Arab sheiks (chiefs) for camels.

Knowing that the food might run out, Eaton also arranged for the U.S. Navy to send a ship filled with relief supplies and weapons to the harbor of Bomba, near Darnah. If the ship failed to arrive, the army would probably starve.

INTO THE DESERT

By March 1805, everything was ready. Early on March 4, the army assembled. Eaton took the lead on an Arabian stallion, followed by about three hundred Arabs, all on horses. The European and American troops, including U.S. Marines dressed in dark blue coats and tall black hats, marched behind. A train of camels and donkeys brought up the rear, with their drivers mulling around to keep them in line and moving.

The army was entering territory conquered more than one thousand years before by Arab armies. An earlier conqueror of the region was the ancient Greek general Alexander the Great. Eaton probably dwelled pleasantly on the fact that he was following in the footsteps of Alexander, but his study of the general's campaigns gave him little detail about the area he was entering. Eaton's maps simply showed blank space. Ahmad Qaramanli had made the journey before, but only once when fleeing from Darnah. The entire army depended on

WILLIAM EATON, AHMAD QARAMANLI, AND THEIR FORCES MARCHED ACROSS 500 MILES (804 KM) OF DESERT TO THE NORTH AFRICAN CITY OF DARNAH IN 1805.

Arab members who were familiar with the region. Only they knew where the wells lay.

The region was mostly desert. The landscape offered shades of gray, brown, and white, broken here and there by patches of grass and the vivid dots of colored flowers. The northern horizon was the dark blue bar of the Mediterranean Sea. A U.S. sailor, Midshipman Pascal Paoli Peck, described the first day's trek "under burning sun." The force camped next to a water hole—but it was dry. No one could refresh themselves that night. "I laid myself down on my bed to sleep but could not, being for the first time in my life almost dead with thirst. Had I possessed thousands I would have given them for [a small amount of] water," wrote Peck.

A Divided Army

A few days into the journey, Eaton hit his first serious snag. One morning the camel drivers refused to go farther unless they received more money. Eaton had promised to pay them when the expedition was complete, but rumors had spread among the drivers that Eaton planned to cheat them. The drivers, who were Muslim, muttered darkly among themselves: who could trust a Christian?

Eaton argued with the drivers through the morning. Neither side yielded. Infuriated, Eaton threatened to cancel the expedition. He abruptly ordered his U.S. Marines and European soldiers to begin retracing the route back to Alexandria. The camel drivers faced a new dilemma. If Eaton canceled the expedition, they would earn nothing. Eaton's tactic worked. The camel drivers backed off and the march resumed. That night Eaton wrote with disgust in his journal, "Money, more money, was the only stimulus that can give motion to the camp."

Two days later, a figure on horseback suddenly appeared. It was a messenger from Darnah, and he brought good news: The people of Darnah had heard that Ahmad Qaramanli was approaching. They were arming themselves and preparing to join in a general rebellion against the governor of the city, who was allied with Yusuf. The governor was so terrified, said the messenger, that he was hiding in his castle.

Some of the Arab horsemen heard this news and began celebrating in a traditional Arab way—by firing guns into the air. At the back of the camel train, the camel drivers heard the shots and thought that local Bedouin tribesmen—fierce tribal warriors—were attacking. Thinking they were about to be captured by Bedouins, the camel drivers decided to switch sides. They moved to kill the force's Christians—

the Europeans and Americans. In response, the Christian soldiers raised their weapons. It appeared that the entire expedition might abruptly end in massacre.

Finally, the drivers learned the true cause of the first shots, and both they and the Christians lowered their weapons. The distrust lingered, however, and the incident showed that Eaton's army was divided. The Christians and Muslims scorned each other and didn't speak or eat together. At night the Christians pitched their tents on one side of the campsite, and the Muslims pitched their tents on the other side. Ahmad Qaramanli slept alone in a special tent made of silk. If William Eaton wondered how these men could fight side by side, he kept it to himself. Presley O'Bannon, for his part, ordered the marines to sleep on their muskets to prevent theft.

DELAYS

The army managed about 25 miles (40 km) per day. Each night they stopped near a well, where water was plentiful. The soldiers' meals were meager, however. In the morning, each received two biscuits, which were supposed to last through the day. At night each man ate a bowl of rice. Eaton posted marines to guard the sacks of rice and beans.

After about 200 miles (322 km), the camel drivers again refused to move. No blustering or threats from Eaton could change their minds. This time, Eaton learned that Ahmad had asked the drivers to carry the expedition only 200 miles, not the full 500 (804 km). Ahmad explained that he had expected to draw more support from his followers in the countryside. He was certain that by then, other Arabs would have provided camels. Eaton was puzzled by Ahmad's reasoning, but he had no time to argue. Realizing that the camel drivers were not going to move, Eaton took a different tack. He agreed to hand over money to them on the spot. Eaton and his officers scrounged up $680, which was distributed to the drivers. They accepted the money with many thanks, and Eaton looked forward to resuming the march.

But that night, more than half the drivers slipped out of camp to return to Egypt. The next morning, the remaining half announced again that they would not move. Eaton stalked back to his tent and pondered his options. He had no more money, and the delays were literally eating into his supplies. His army was running out of food.

That night the rest of the camel drivers abandoned the camp. In the morning, the sheiks of the Arab cavalry said that they too would march no farther. They had heard rumors that Yusuf had raised an army of more than fifteen hundred cavalry and foot soldiers. This force was marching to Darnah.

Ahmad and the sheiks met in a tent to decide what to do next. They debated throughout the day while Eaton stewed. Eaton finally got an invitation to join them at midnight. He entered the tent, where the council again told him that they would not march any farther. The sheiks wanted to send a runner 300 miles (483 km) ahead to Bomba to be sure the relief ship would be waiting for them.

Eaton's response was brief. He told the council that anyone not joining the march would not receive food. Without another word, Eaton turned and left. The next morning, his U.S. Marines and European soldiers stood guard over the rice sacks. Eaton waited for a response.

The Arab leaders gave in. By noon about fifty of the camels had reappeared, and the march resumed. Two days later, the force stumbled into a vast Bedouin camp. The Bedouins often attacked outsiders, but this tribe despised Yusuf Qaramanli and supported Ahmad. They welcomed Eaton's army, and about eighty Bedouin warriors pledged to fight with them.

Eaton was delighted with this addition and gave orders to march in the morning. That day, however, a messenger arrived to say that Yusuf's army was just a few days' march from Darnah. Again, this news unsettled the Arabs. Ahmad appeared stricken with fear. The camel drivers began to retreat, and the sheiks plotted to return to Egypt. Again, Eaton ordered his European soldiers and U.S. Marines to guard the food.

TO THE BRINK

The crisis passed, happened again, and passed again. Eaton grew frustrated. After several weeks of marches and delays, the army reached a sandy plateau and the landscape turned drier. Centuries before, people had dug wells deep into the rock at regular intervals. Travelers relied on the pools of freshwater inside the dark wells to survive in the harsh terrain. Eaton and his army were no different. The men and animals, exhausted after a day of marching, looked forward to drinking the water each night.

On April 5, after a 12-mile (19 km) march, the men came to a well and found it dry. Another well nearby had water, but it smelled of sulfur. Some men pinched their noses and sipped it anyway, but the water made them sick. The army pressed on early the next morning. They found another well, but its water was muddy. The men and animals drank what they could and moved on. That night the army camped in a spot without any freshwater.

The army set out at sunrise and soon stretched into a long line of exhausted men and animals. The men carefully sipped their last reserves of water from goatskin bags. The animals had not drunk anything in two days. That night, Eaton called a halt. The new campsite had no well. No water.

The situation was serious. Within a day, most of the animals would start dying, and the men would soon follow. The force had gone too far down the trail to turn back. The only hope was that a well would be found ahead. Presley O'Bannon had cheerfully claimed that he would follow William Eaton to hell. O'Bannon might have thought that he had arrived precisely there. With visions of refreshment tormenting their thoughts, the men set out again at dawn.

They marched three hours down a mountainside into a ravine. There they saw fresh rainwater gushing into a well. The men and animals joyfully crowded around to drink. Once the men were satisfied, Eaton ordered the march to resume. The Arabs, however, had already pitched camp. They refused to move until they found out whether the U.S. relief ship was at Bomba. Eaton passionately argued that the expedition had to move quickly. They were almost out of food. To delay any further would put them all at risk of starvation. To make his point, Eaton cut the Arabs off from their rice rations. Ahmad and the sheiks held another council. After several hours, Ahmad emerged and confronted Eaton. He said the sheiks had decided not to follow through with the attack and would retreat to Egypt. Eaton watched as the Arabs pulled down their tents and loaded their camels. A rumor spread that the Arabs planned to steal the rice before they began their journey. Eaton ordered his men to grab their muskets and form companies in front of the supply camp. The lines of Europeans and U.S. Marines, no more than sixty individuals altogether, stood silently.

Eaton's Notebook

MODERN HISTORIANS HAVE A wonderfully detailed account of William Eaton's adventure in the North African desert because Eaton faithfully kept a journal. Almost every night, no matter how exhausted he was, Eaton chronicled the events of the day. However, Eaton's account is the only one we have. Except for a few letters written by U.S. sailors, no other perspective on the trek has survived. It would be particularly interesting if Ahmad Qaramanli or an Arab sheik had kept a diary. Such an account might differ markedly from Eaton's version of events.

Around them milled hundreds of Arabs, making final preparations to leave. The Arabs left in groups, and soon they were gone.

Eaton and his sixty-man army stayed in the ravine. Eaton hoped that the Arabs, having no food for their journey, would return. Within an hour, Eaton's hunch proved correct. Ahmad returned with the sheiks and other Arabs in tow, explaining that he had persuaded the sheiks to rejoin the expedition. Tensions remained high, but the march continued.

TO BOMBA

Bomba now lay 50 to 60 miles (80 to 97 km) away. The rice ration had dwindled to 4 ounces (113 grams) per man per day—a mere handful—and this would last only three more days. On the forty-first day of the journey, the men ate the last grains of rice. The sacks were empty, and Bomba was still days away. The hungry men slaughtered one of their camels and eagerly consumed the hundreds of pounds of meat. The army struggled on for the next two days without food. Some of the men scraped aside the desert soil to find edible roots.

Finally, on a late afternoon, the army climbed a hill that overlooked the harbor at Bomba. From there, they saw the sand meet the water's edge—and the harbor was empty. No ships. Frantically, the men scanned the sea for a glimpse of a sail—but saw only the hard blue line of the horizon.

The realization was crushing. The Arab soldiers cursed loudly, proclaiming that the whole expedition had been a trick. "They abused us as imposters and infidels [non-Muslims]," recalled Eaton, "and said we had drawn them into that situation with treacherous views." Ahmad and the sheiks again called a conference and excluded Eaton once again. Desperate, Eaton forced himself into the tent. This time, he did not bluster. He told the sheiks to march immediately and attack Darnah. But Ahmad and the sheiks announced that they were pulling out the next morning.

Eaton told the Arabs that a ship was coming. As a last gesture, Eaton, the marines, and the European soldiers built a large signal fire on a hill overlooking the harbor. They tended the fire through the night, but at dawn, the harbor was still empty. The disgusted Muslims packed up their camels and prepared to leave. A long line of men, horses, and camels began the long trek back to Egypt.

At eight in the morning, Ahmad's treasurer climbed up the hill and approached Eaton. He had grown fond of the American and wanted to bid him farewell personally. Suddenly, he noticed a white speck on the horizon. He looked carefully. A sail! "Language is too poor to paint the joy and exultation which this messenger of life painted in every breast," Eaton wrote.

Slowly but surely, the speck grew larger. It was *Argus*, captained by Isaac Hull. The Arabs returned and crowded the hill overlooking the harbor, marveling at the ship. Eaton rolled up his pants and waded into the surf to welcome the sailors who rowed ashore in a small boat. Supplies of food and drink followed, and the tired, famished men enjoyed a luxurious meal that night.

> *"Language is too poor to paint the joy and exultation which [the ship's appearance on the horizon] painted in every breast."*
> —William Eaton, 1805

Victory and Betrayal in Tripoli

While the troops ate and rested for three days, Eaton remained in his tent, planning the attack on Darnah—then just 40 miles (64 km) away. Eaton asked Hull, who commanded *Argus* and another ship, *Hornet*, to support his attack. Eaton wanted Hull to guide his ships close to Darnah and blast the city's walls with large cannons.

The army marched toward Darnah, and within a few days, the city came into sight. It sat at the bottom of a valley on a harbor that faced the Mediterranean. The valley was fertile and filled with crops and fruit trees.

Eaton closely observed the target. His expedition had not caught the Darnah defenders by surprise. They had erected a rough line of earthen walls on the city's northeast side as a defense against Eaton's army. The other side of the city was a wall of houses. Eight cannons overlooked the harbor. A spy informed Eaton that the governor of Darnah commanded about eight hundred men. They manned the defensive wall and had poked holes through the walls of buildings for inserting muskets. The governor appeared confident that he could hold off Eaton's army until Yusuf's relief force arrived. The next morning, Eaton sent a letter to the governor, requesting that his forces be allowed to occupy and pass through the city. The governor's response was brief: "My head or yours."

Eaton prepared to attack. Three ships—*Argus, Hornet,* and a Turkish ship that Hull had captured—supported the attack. Together, the three ships carried almost thirty guns. While these guns pounded Darnah, Eaton would storm the town in a two-pronged assault. He and his Christian troops would strike from the southeast, charging the defenders behind their earthen fortifications. Ahmad, leading several hundred Arab cavalry, would swoop around the city and enter from the other side.

On April 27, at about two in the afternoon, Eaton and his force of Europeans and marines advanced toward the city. The sound of cannons thundered in the harbor as the U.S. ships lobbed shells at Darnah's defenses. Ahmad's cavalry rode around the city and easily seized an old castle at the city's edge. Then they stopped.

In the southeastern corner of the city, Eaton's force was under heavy pressure. The defenders fired muskets at Eaton's men, pinning them down in the open. Musket balls whistled through the air around the soldiers.

By three thirty, with Ahmad stalled, Eaton feared that his own force was losing discipline. After a few more minutes under fire, the men might start to break ranks and flee. Although he was facing a far larger force protected by an earthen wall, Eaton made a bold decision—charge! A drummer boy pounded out the order, and Eaton's command went up and down the line. His men attached sharp-tipped

FINALLY, AFTER TWO MONTHS OF MARCHING ACROSS THE NORTH
AFRICAN DESERT, U.S. MARINES AND THEIR ARAB ALLIES
REACHED THEIR INTENDED TARGET. THEY ATTACKED THE CITY
OF DARNAH ON APRIL 27, 1805.

metal bayonets to their muskets. The drummer boy sounded the
order again. The bugler took up the call. Eaton lunged forward. The
marines followed and then the Europeans. In a jumbled rush, the
force screamed a war cry and surged toward the enemy positions.

The enemy lines exploded with clouds of musket fire. One U.S.
Marine staggered and fell dead, shot through the heart. Another marine
lurched and tumbled down, followed by several European soldiers.
Eaton suddenly winced—a musket ball had smashed through his left
wrist. By then the screaming group had almost reached the earthen
wall. Before the defenders could reload their weapons, the soldiers were
upon them. The defenders broke ranks and ran back into the city.

The surviving U.S. Marines hurried through the maze of streets, dodging gunfire from buildings. They scrambled to a fort, abandoned by its defenders, and lowered the enemy flag. Eaton caught up to them. He pulled out a U.S. flag and ran it up the pole—the first time in history that a U.S. flag had been raised over enemy territory.

The marines then turned the fort's own guns on the city's defenders, while Ahmad's cavalry began to pour into the city. Caught between streams of gunfire and the Arab cavalry, Darnah's defenses quickly collapsed. Scarcely a half hour after Eaton had ordered his reckless charge, the city surrendered.

That night Eaton wrote a letter to his commander, Commodore Samuel Barron, describing the victory. To Eaton's surprise, Barron ordered Eaton to cut off support for Ahmad Qaramanli. The prince had regained Darnah, Barron said. Why could he not muster the support to unseat Yusuf on his own?

Barron wanted the Americans to stop fighting and begin negotiating for peace and the release of the U.S. prisoners. He ordered Tobias Lear, the U.S. representative in Tripoli, to meet with Yusuf Qaramanli. Barron believed that Yusuf had no choice but to listen. He was in

Song and Sword

THE BATTLE OF TRIPOLI became a cherished part of U.S. Marine Corps history. "The Marines' Hymn" begins with the line "From the halls of Montezuma to the shores of Tripoli." In addition, every marine dressed in formal uniform carries a sword. The sword is fashioned after a scimitar that Ahmad Qaramanli gave to Lieutenant Presley O'Bannon.

trouble. The loss of Darnah had been devastating. He had no more money and couldn't even afford to feed his servants and bodyguards more than one meal a day.

In Tripoli, city residents were tired of Yusuf Qaramanli's rule and also believed they were losing the war against the Americans. Rumors claimed that a fleet of sixty U.S. ships was coming to blast the city into rubble. An eyewitness heard Yusuf say that "if it were in his power to make peace and give up the U.S. prisoners, he would gladly do it without the consideration of money."

Tobias Lear proved to be an easier negotiator than Yusuf deserved. When he approached Tripoli harbor, he had little idea how desperate for peace Yusuf and his people were. Negotiations moved quickly. Yusuf asked for sixty thousand dollars as payment for the U.S. prisoners and two gunboats. His main request, however, was that Ahmad abandon Darnah. Lear, who had never supported Eaton's campaign, accepted these terms. Worse for Ahmad, Lear secretly agreed that Yusuf could keep Ahmad's family captive for another four years. With the agreement completed on June 3, the war between Tripoli and the United States officially ended.

Eaton was still in Darnah, unaware of the negotiations. He refused to leave the city until he received clear orders from Barron. On June 11, the giant, three-masted frigate USS *Constellation* arrived outside Darnah. It brought Eaton the crushing news that the United States and Tripoli had signed a peace treaty.

Eaton was infuriated when he heard the terms. How could the United States abandon Ahmad in favor of the pirate Yusuf? Letting Yusuf escape, he argued, reinforced the entire pirate system. He also noted that pulling out of Darnah would mean abandoning those Arabs who had supported the United States. Yusuf's troops had by then arrived outside Darnah. Once Eaton's army left, they would quickly take over the city and massacre anyone who had supported Ahmad.

As for the sixty thousand dollars, Eaton thought the United States should have paid no money whatsoever. He later wrote that Darnah was home to twelve thousand inhabitants. "Could this [city] not have been exchanged for 200 prisoners of war? Was the attempt made?" he asked with disgust. "We gave a kingdom for peace."

Eaton broke the news to Ahmad. There was nothing they could do but evacuate Darnah. They would have to leave the Arab armies behind, probably to face death at the hands of Yusuf's forces. Ahmad and Eaton kept the plans in total secrecy—if news leaked out, the Arab forces would certainly kill them for the betrayal.

On the night of June 12, Eaton secretly loaded the Christian soldiers and marines onto rowboats bound for *Constellation*. Ahmad, with forty of his close followers, also fled to the ship. Around midnight, Eaton left the fort and joined the evacuees. When his boat was about 50 yards (46 m) offshore, he heard the shrieks and curses of Arab soldiers and Darnah citizens. They had discovered the betrayal.

Fallout from the Treaty

The release of the U.S. prisoners from Tripoli brought joy to Americans, but it also raised questions—mostly regarding the terms Lear had negotiated with Yusuf Qaramanli. At that time, the Democratic Party, led by President Jefferson, and the Federalist Party dominated U.S. politics. The Federalists were angry at the peace terms, believing that Lear could have driven a harder bargain.

When Eaton returned to the United States in early November 1805, he was in a foul mood. He brooded over what he believed was a disgraceful treaty. He was most disgusted with how the United States had treated its ally Ahmad Qaramanli.

Eaton's mood brightened somewhat after he arrived. As he made his way up the eastern seaboard to Washington, D.C., residents of the cities along the way lauded him. Leading citizens made toasts in his honor and, noting his wounded wrist, commended his bravery. "Almost everyone was anxious to see or to tell of the appearance of Eaton," wrote the *Richmond Enquirer* breathlessly. "His eye is brilliant and full of fire." When Eaton arrived in Washington, he was the center of attention.

Eaton strongly criticized Tobias Lear, calling him "jealous, cowardly, and what was worse—false." He became enraged when he learned that Lear had made a secret agreement with Yusuf to keep Ahmad's family in captivity for four more years. Eaton was mortified, calling the agreement with Yusuf a "national disgrace."

Eaton wrote letters to President Jefferson, requesting justice for Ahmad. By this time, however, Jefferson could not be bothered. A British ship had fired upon a U.S. ship just off the coast of Virginia. The British captain claimed the right to stop the U.S. ship and search for sailors who had deserted the British navy. Washington, D.C., was full of angry war talk. No one in this environment cared to listen to William Eaton's claims of poor treatment or hear about Ahmad Qaramanli's misery.

THE END OF THE PIRATE COAST

While William Eaton waged his futile fight, U.S. relations with the Barbary States were mostly peaceful. Meanwhile, Great Britain continued to stop U.S. ships at sea in search of deserters. In the process, the

British also seized many U.S. sailors and forced them to serve in the British navy. Angered by this practice and other British policies, President James Madison declared war on Great Britain on June 1, 1812.

The War of 1812 did not turn out as either side had hoped. The U.S. Navy, led by its powerful frigates, battered three British frigates into surrender. These victories astonished the British people. On the other hand, the U.S. Army performed poorly. A British army terrorized the region around the Chesapeake Bay in Virginia and was able to capture and burn parts of Washington, D.C.

As the war dragged on, the British asked the Barbary pirates to resume attacks on U.S. merchant ships. In Algiers the dey declared war on the United States. Once again, Algerine pirates cruised the Mediterranean, looking for U.S. ships. The pirates captured one ship and enslaved its ten-man crew.

Great Britain and the United States finally made peace in 1815. The end of war freed Americans to turn their attention back to the Barbary Coast. When the treaty with Great Britain was just one week old, President Madison asked Congress to fund a force that would sail to the Mediterranean Sea and crush the pirates once and for all. By then confident commanders led the battle-tested U.S. Navy. Congress immediately agreed and declared war on the Barbary States.

In May 1815, Commodore Stephen Decatur led a U.S. squadron into the Mediterranean, determined to settle old scores. He sailed first to Algiers. Along the way, he captured the forty-six-gun Algerine warship *Meshuda* and killed its admiral. In Algiers, Decatur delivered Madison's declaration of war to the dey. He also gave the dey conditions for peace: all U.S. prisoners to be released immediately, all U.S. property in the city returned, and ten thousand dollars in cash. The dey tried to haggle another deal, but Decatur stated that he would not negotiate. After a few days, the dey agreed to the U.S. terms.

Decatur sailed on eastward to the next Barbary State, Tunis. He arrived in the harbor and demanded forty-six thousand dollars in cash for the loss of two ships during the War of 1812. When the Tunisian leader, called the bey, asked for more time, Decatur refused. Like the dey in Algiers, the bey of Tunis knew that he had no options. He paid the bill, and the Americans sailed on to Tripoli.

Yusuf Qaramanli was still on the throne in Tripoli. During the War of 1812, he had seized two U.S. ships and given them to the British, violating his treaty with the Americans. Decatur demanded twenty-five thousand dollars in compensation. Yusuf tried to bargain, but again Decatur would not consider it. Yusuf complained but soon paid.

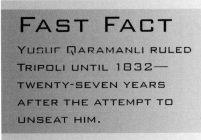

FAST FACT

YUSUF QARAMANLI RULED TRIPOLI UNTIL 1832— TWENTY-SEVEN YEARS AFTER THE ATTEMPT TO UNSEAT HIM.

The U.S. example shamed the other European countries, who realized they no longer needed to pay off the Barbary pirates. In 1816 a British and Dutch naval force bombarded Algerine fortifications into rubble. Algiers surrendered. Tunis and Tripoli soon agreed to treaties that stated they would never seize Christian slaves again.

CHAPTER 4

More Small Wars

A SAILOR WROTE at the time of the Barbary Wars, "The mention of Tripoli calls up proud recollection of the infancy of the U.S. Navy. It was upon the coast of that country, that Americans began to learn how to conquer upon the sea." The navy matured during the War of 1812. During the early years of that war, a separate, little-known conflict took place in the South Pacific Ocean.

The war began after the thirty-two-gun frigate USS *Essex*, having fought the British in the Atlantic, sailed around the tip of South America into the Pacific Ocean. Its commander was Captain David Porter, a fierce and demanding officer trained by Edward Preble. The first U.S. warship to enter the Pacific, *Essex* attacked and captured several British merchant ships. In October 1813, Porter looked for a safe port to refit *Essex*, which badly needed repairs after many months at sea.

Porter feared that British ships would capture *Essex* if he stayed in a South American port. Instead, Porter decided to sail west—more than 2,500 miles (4,022 km)—to a chain of South Pacific islands called the Marquesas. On October 25, *Essex* arrived in the largest of the Marquesas, Nuka Hiva. With the U.S. ship were four captured British merchant ships and several British sailors.

Nuka Hiva appeared to be a tropical paradise. Steep mountains covered in a lush green matting of vines and trees surrounded the harbor. The sailors were delighted to mingle with the local tribe, the Taaehs. The chief of the

CAPTAIN DAVID PORTER HAD BEEN TO TRIPOLI WITH THE U.S. MISSION TO THE AREA IN 1801. HE WAS TAKEN PRISONER DURING THE ATTACK ON THE *PHILADELPHIA* AND WAS RELEASED IN 1805. HE WAS IN CHARGE OF THE U.S. NAVAL CONFLICT IN THE SOUTH PACIFIC OCEAN IN 1813.

Taaehs allowed the Americans to camp on his beach—but only if they helped the Taaehs fight another tribe, the Happahs.

Porter did not want to get entangled in local quarrels, but the chief's request was impossible to ignore. Porter sent a small force of Americans into the mountains to confront the Happahs. After a brief but bloody skirmish, the Happahs asked for peace.

Secure on the island, Porter built a small town for his men—called

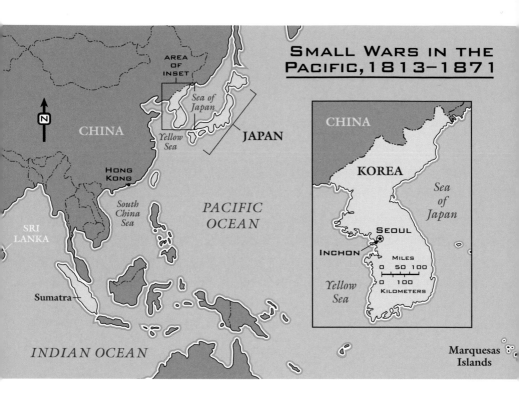

Madisonville after President James Madison—with a small fort. The sailors raised a U.S. flag over the fort, and Porter claimed the island for the United States. He hoped the base would provide support for future U.S. naval operations in the area.

Then Porter received bad news. Yet another tribe on the island—the Typee—threatened the Americans, calling them "white lizards, mere dirt." Porter organized a force of five thousand reconciled Taaehs and Happahs and led them to attack the Typee. The mixed army landed near the Typee village but retreated under a hail of spears and stones. This defeat led to a collapse of prestige. When Porter retreated to Madisonville, he worried that the Taaehs and Happahs would turn on him and massacre his sailors.

Porter organized another attack. This time, the Americans marched around the Typee village and descended from a steep mountainside. Porter sent a message that he would destroy the entire village unless the Typee surrendered. Receiving no response, the Americans attacked and burned the village. Seeing their huts reduced to a "long line of smoking ruins," the Typee agreed to peace.

Madisonville didn't last. Porter sailed with *Essex* in December, bound for South America. He left twenty-one U.S. sailors and a few British prisoners to hold the fort. He also left the four British merchant ships behind. On May 7, 1814, the British prisoners seized one of the merchant ships and disappeared into the open sea. Two days later, the Taaehs attacked and killed four U.S. sailors on the beach. The survivors fled to one of the remaining merchant ships and escaped from the harbor, never to return.

The U.S. venture into the Marquesas was one of the nation's forgotten small wars. David Porter was ahead of his time. He wanted to claim new territory for the United States. Most Americans of this era, however, disagreed with that desire. They believed that seizing overseas territory was un-American. But as U.S. naval power grew, that idea began to change.

SEA POWER

U.S. victories against the ships of the British navy—the greatest navy in the world—gave Americans enormous pride after the War of 1812. The captains of the victorious ships became household names. Congress's previous debates about the cost and dangers of maintaining a navy faded from memory.

After the war ended, President Madison asked Congress to finance a long-term naval construction program. With little debate, Congress agreed. At the cost of $1 million per year for eight years, the government built nine ships of the line and twelve heavy frigates.

In 1823 President James Monroe announced what came to be known as the Monroe Doctrine. At that time, European countries had long been colonizing territories in other parts of the world. For instance, France, Great Britain, and other nations had seized control of lands and natural resources in Africa and Asia. In the Monroe Doctrine, the president declared that the United States would consider any further European expansion into the Western Hemisphere (North, Central, and South America) a hostile act. Over the next several decades, the Europeans respected the Monroe Doctrine—mostly because of U.S. naval power.

Having established its dominance in the Western Hemisphere, the United States began to show its strength farther abroad. One conflict came in the 1830s on the island of Sumatra, part of modern-day Indonesia. U.S. merchants had long traded with Sumatra for pepper, a valuable spice. The trade was mostly profitable for both sides, although Sumatran pirates sometimes attacked and plundered U.S. merchant ships.

THE FIFTH PRESIDENT OF THE UNITED STATES, JAMES MONROE, FORMULATED THE MONROE DOCTRINE IN 1823.

In 1831 pirates swarmed over the U.S. merchant vessel *Friendship* and killed several sailors. The surviving crew, still onshore, fled to another harbor, where several other U.S. merchant ships came to their aid. The men recovered the *Friendship*, but its cargo, worth forty thousand dollars, was gone.

One of the shipowners was a U.S. senator. He complained to President Andrew Jackson, who ordered a forty-four-gun U.S. warship, *Potomac*, to sail to Sumatra and punish the pirates. *Potomac*, commanded by Jack Downes, slipped into a Sumatran harbor disguised as a Dutch merchant ship. Onshore was a Sumatran village with four thousand inhabitants and four forts. Downes had orders to meet with the Sumatrans and seek a peaceful resolution to the piracy. However, Downes decided simply to attack.

At dawn on February 6, 1832, almost three hundred marines and sailors stormed ashore while *Potomac*'s guns thundered overhead. The Sumatran defenders came out with swords and spears. The marines scattered this force and captured three forts. The remaining fort held out for a day, until Downes steered *Potomac* near the shore and fired several broadsides directly into the structure. Under this pressure, the Sumatrans surrendered and promised never to harm Americans again.

Downes requested payment for the loss of *Friendship*'s cargo, but the Sumatrans refused. Considering his point made, Downes did not push the matter. He and *Potomac* left for China. The short, savage action had left two Americans dead and several wounded and killed about one hundred Sumatrans.

Back in the United States, many Americans criticized Downes for attacking before attempting to negotiate. They also wondered why, after so much bloodshed, Downes had won no payment for *Friendship*'s cargo.

Marine Corps History

THE U.S. MARINE CORPS is one of the nation's elite fighting organizations. It dates to 1775 and the American Revolution, when Congress authorized the formation of two marine battalions. The marines at that time were posted aboard naval ships. Through the nineteenth century, marines mostly served as land forces for the navy. They splashed ashore to protect U.S. citizens, property, and interests in dozens of foreign lands.

This role changed in the twentieth century. During the first decades of the 1900s, the marines served as fast-reacting forces, ready for deployment in any part of the world. They were among the first U.S. forces to see action in World War I. During World War II, the marines grew rapidly in size. They assaulted Japanese-held islands in the Pacific and saw some of the most savage fighting in U.S. history. The modern marines are small compared to the other branches of the armed forces. But they are also the best known and carry one of the best reputations of any armed force in the world.

Moreover, the expedition did not result in peace for U.S. merchant ships in Indonesia. In 1838 Sumatran pirates attacked another U.S. ship, *Eclipse*. The pirates killed some crew members and forced others to swim for their lives. Two U.S. naval ships, the frigate *Columbia* and sloop *John Adams*, were in nearby Sri Lanka when the attack occurred. This small fleet, commanded by Captain George C. Read, arrived off Sumatra in late December.

This time, Read was careful to first attempt to negotiate with the Sumatrans. When these talks failed, Read ordered an attack. His ships bombarded the same forts that had been captured five years before. The Sumatrans soon offered two thousand dollars as compensation to the *Eclipse* owners and agreed, once again, to leave U.S. shipping alone.

Numerous small wars followed the Sumatran conflicts. In fact, between 1841 and 1861, the U.S. Marines landed in foreign countries twenty-four times. The Mexican War (1846–1848) marked the first time the United States invaded and defeated a foreign country and then kept some of its territory. Other nations ignored the United States at their own peril.

One nation that initially resisted U.S. power was Japan, an island country in the North Pacific Ocean. In the first half of the nineteenth century, Japan mostly closed its borders to trade with the United States and other Western nations. Japanese leaders wanted no contact with the West, which they considered a threat to their society and rule. The West, on the other hand, saw great profits to be made in trading with Japan.

In 1853 Commodore Matthew Perry led a fleet of four U.S. naval ships to the Japanese coast. He demanded that Japanese leaders read and reply to a letter from U.S. president Millard Fillmore, who proposed peace, friendship, and trade between the United States and Japan. Perry threatened a bombardment if Japan refused the offer. Seeing the powerful U.S. ships,

COMMODORE MATTHEW PERRY SERVED IN THE U.S. NAVY FROM 1809 TO 1855. HE WENT TO JAPAN IN 1853 TO MEET WITH JAPANESE LEADERS ABOUT A TRADE DEAL.

THE CREW OF THE USS *MONITOR* STANDS ON DECK IN JULY 1862 DURING THE AMERICAN CIVIL WAR. THE *MONITOR* WAS AN IRONCLAD SHIP, COVERED IN IRON ARMOR PLATES. THIS NEW TYPE OF POWERFUL SHIP PLAYED A BIG ROLE IN DEFEATING THE CONFEDERACY.

the Japanese realized that they were overmatched militarily and agreed to a trade treaty, opening up Japan to Western influence.

THE NAVY'S DARK AGES

During the Civil War (1861–1865), U.S. small wars mostly stopped, because the great conflict between North and South absorbed all the energies of the nation's military forces. During the war, the northern-controlled U.S. Navy overwhelmed the much smaller Confederate (Southern) navy. Through the war, the U.S. Navy grew enormously.

When the Civil War ended, however, the U.S. quickly dismantled its great fleet. Just ten years after the war, Great Britain published a survey of the world's navies. The U.S. fleet ranked low on the list, below the navies of Brazil, Turkey, and Austria.

Americans paid little attention to issues outside their borders in the post–Civil War years. They instead devoted their energies to expanding westward and building factories in their growing cities. The U.S. Navy was neglected, leading to a period that naval historians would later call the navy's "dark ages."

A few small wars occurred during this era, however. In the early 1870s, Rear Admiral John Rodgers commanded the U.S. Asiatic Squadron based in Hong Kong, a British-held port on the coast of China. With the six ships under his command, Rodgers believed that he could open nearby Korea to foreign trade. Commodore Perry had used his ships and cannons to force Japan to open up, and Rodgers hoped to win similar glory.

For their part, Korea's rulers were determined to keep their nation closed to foreign influence. In 1871 Rodgers led an expedition of five ships and twelve hundred men to change the Koreans' minds.

The Fate of the Six Frigates

THE SIX FRIGATES ORIGINALLY built in response to the Barbary pirates—the *Constitution, Chesapeake, Constellation, Congress, President,* and *United States*—became part of U.S. naval mythology. The stories of the ships, their battles, their captains, and their crews circulated for many years. As the ships aged and finally were retired and scrapped, officers and sailors saved tiny pieces as souvenirs.

At the end of May, the force arrived at the Korean port of Inchon. Rodgers sent several small ships up the Han River toward the capital city of Seoul to establish contact with Korea's rulers. The Koreans saw the ships as invaders and opened fire.

When Korea refused to apologize for the incident, Rodgers ordered his force to land and attack. The Americans took two Korean forts quickly. A third rested high on a ridge. The Americans stormed it. A wild and bloody hand-to-hand fight followed that left three hundred Korean defenders dead. Only three Americans died in the operation, and fifteen marines and sailors earned Medals of Honor for their efforts.

IN 1871 ADMIRAL JOHN RODGERS ATTEMPTED TO FORCE KOREA TO OPEN UP TO U.S. TRADE AS JAPAN HAD DONE. THE CAMPAIGN DID NOT GO AS WELL.

Rodgers believed he had made his point and believed the Koreans would negotiate, so he ordered his men to reboard their ships. But three weeks later, the Koreans still would not talk. Not wanting to invade the entire country, Rodgers withdrew. Korea claimed that it had repulsed the Western invaders, but the battle had, in fact, strongly favored the Americans. Within the next decade, Korea did open up to the outside world, signing treaties with both Japan and the United States.

New Debates

By 1880 the United States had grown vastly from its origins as a string of colonies along the eastern seaboard of North America. The country had expanded overland to the Pacific Ocean. Its cities were growing. Millions of immigrants, eager for jobs and freedom, arrived each year in ships from Europe and Asia. The country was bursting with the energy of growth and expansion.

Many Americans argued over the U.S. role in the world. The nation had become very powerful—but how should it use that power? Some argued that the United States should simply mind its own affairs. European nations had already colonized much of the world, exploiting both the citizens and natural resources of poorer nations. The United States, which considered itself a great democracy, should not engage in colonialism, they said.

Others argued the opposite. They believed that the United States had the right—the duty—to project its strength onto the world. They said the nation should take its rightful place among the other great naval powers of the day. One of the most vocal supporters of this view was a young, brilliant man named Theodore Roosevelt.

CHAPTER 5

The Big Stick

THEODORE (TEDDY) ROOSEVELT, the son of a New York businessman, had a long-standing interest in ships. He recalled that during his childhood, his mother had told him stories about his uncle, a shipbuilder. She would talk "about ships, ships, ships, and fighting of ships till they sank into the depths of my soul," Roosevelt later said.

As a student at Harvard University, he began writing about naval warfare, although his professors wished he would focus more on languages and mathematics. "My mind was running to ships that were fighting each other," he later recalled. Shortly after he graduated from Harvard, Roosevelt decided to write a history of the naval battles of the War of 1812.

The twenty-three-year-old spent hours in the study of his family's New York City home, researching the first ships of the U.S. Navy. He diagrammed the movements of ships on paper, tracing their maneuvers during battle. His young wife complained, "We're dining out in twenty minutes, and Teddy's drawing little ships!"

Roosevelt's book *The Naval War of 1812* appeared in 1882. Critics hailed its excellent scholarship and its thoroughness. In one short section, Roosevelt wrote about the weak state of the U.S. Navy in the 1880s. "It is folly," he wrote, "for the great English-speaking Republic to rely for defense upon a navy composed partly of antiquated hulks and partly of new vessels rather more worthless than the old."

ASSISTANT SECRETARY

By 1897, fifteen years after sounding the alarm about the state of the navy, Theodore Roosevelt had become one of the most recognizable politicians in the United States. Wearing spectacles and flashing a toothy grin, the thirty-seven-year-old had held city, state, and federal offices. On April 19, 1897, Roosevelt became assistant secretary of the U.S. Navy.

Roosevelt had little first-hand knowledge of the navy. He had never served on

THEODORE ROOSEVELT (PHOTOGRAPHED HERE IN 1899) HAD GREAT PLANS FOR THE U.S. NAVY WHEN HE BECAME ITS ASSISTANT SECRETARY IN 1897.

a ship, and he preferred horseback riding to sailing. But he had already demonstrated a fierce interest in naval history and had also established himself in government as a man who could get things done. Moreover, he was well known in the U.S. Navy. Most of its officers had read his *Naval War of 1812*.

Equipped with a photographic memory and a childlike enthusiasm, Roosevelt moved into his Washington, D.C., office, which held a prime view of the White House lawn, and went eagerly to work. Roosevelt's views of the importance of naval power had not mellowed with time. If anything, they had strengthened.

In the 1880s and 1890s, the United States had grown—in wealth, in population, and in size. In addition, the nation had settled its vast western lands. Many Americans, including Roosevelt, believed that the nation should keep expanding. They envisioned a U.S. empire extending over the island of Cuba in the Caribbean Sea, and the islands of Hawaii and other territories in the Pacific Ocean. Making the situation more urgent, European powers and Japan seemed just as eager to establish or expand their empires.

"IMMENSE FUN"

As the assistant secretary of the navy, Roosevelt served under the secretary, a genial man named John D. Long. Long's greatest quality appeared to be a civilized kindness. Roosevelt called him a "gentleman" and a "perfect dear," although it is not clear whether Roosevelt intended a tone of mockery. Next to Roosevelt, who embodied force and action, Long seemed like an elderly man awaking from a nap.

Long had no deep passion for the U.S. Navy, and unlike

Roosevelt, he did not have a mind that could absorb and analyze reams of statistics and diagrams. Most agreeable to Roosevelt, Long did not appear to disapprove as Roosevelt took on more and more of the administration of the navy himself. After one week on the job, Roosevelt had memorized the condition of the U.S. fleet— where its ships were stationed, its supplies, its repair schedules, and its ammunition. He quickly sent a letter to the president, William McKinley, updating him on the status of the U.S. warships and warning him of potential trouble spots, especially Cuba.

Spain ruled Cuba, as it had since shortly after the voyages of Christopher Columbus more than four centuries before. The island nation sits just 90 miles (145 km) off the coast of Florida in the Caribbean Sea. On a clear day, residents of Key West, Florida, can see all the way to Cuba.

Throughout U.S. history, various Americans had called for the United States to conquer and annex Cuba. Few took these calls seriously, and many argued that the United States had no business establishing an empire. To Theodore Roosevelt and a new generation of Americans, however, Cuba was irresistible. They argued that the Cuban people, who lived in poverty and oppression under Spain, would welcome U.S. rule and the U.S. system of justice.

Just seven weeks after taking office as assistant secretary of the navy, Roosevelt gave a speech that became the talk of the nation. The location was the Naval War College in Newport, Rhode Island, where Roosevelt addressed a class of naval officers. The theme of his speech was simple: preparation for war was the best way to preserve peace, and the best way to prepare for war was to maintain a strong navy. He then thundered that the U.S. Navy had fallen behind those of other nations—Great Britain, Spain, Germany, and Japan.

Modernizing the Navy

FOR THOUSANDS OF YEARS, sailors relied on wind and oars to propel their wooden ships around the world. In the 1850s, however, navies began to replace their wooden ships with ships made of steel and iron and driven by giant steam engines. The age of sail was over.

New, modern ships with metal hulls cruised through the world's seas, with plumes of smoke rising from their coal-fired engines. The modernization also included machine-loaded guns. No longer did sailors have to stuff gunpowder and shells into the mouths of cannons during battle.

He warned that the current situation was dire. It took years to build sophisticated, modern battleships made of steel and iron. In the event of a war, the United States would be hopelessly behind, unable to modernize fast enough to cope with a better-armed foe. "Since the change in military conditions in modern times," he explained, "there has never been an instance in which a war between two nations has lasted more than two years. In most recent wars, the operations *of the first ninety days* have decided the results of the conflict."

Roosevelt's logic was irresistible. The country needed a modern navy and needed it fast. Roosevelt's speech also promoted war— repeatedly. He roared that "all the great masterful races have been fighting races; and the minute that a race loses the hard fighting virtues, then it has lost its proud right to stand as the equal of the best."

Roosevelt's speech was shocking in its forcefulness and its embrace of the glory of war. "It is too late to prepare for war when the time of peace has passed," Roosevelt warned the nation, and the nation was ready to listen. As a new century approached, many Americans came to believe that the United States did have interests outside its borders. They agreed with Roosevelt's claim that the U.S. Navy was the best tool to defend those interests.

Roosevelt's speech did not impress Secretary Long. He saw little need for a buildup and was stunned to hear his subordinate proclaim the importance of the navy. Long turned a deaf ear to Roosevelt's arguments. But he trusted his assistant enough to leave him in charge of the navy when he abandoned the summer heat of Washington for a two-month vacation.

> *"It is too late to prepare for war when the time of peace has passed."*
> —Theodore Roosevelt, 1897

With his boss out of town, Roosevelt swiftly began issuing orders to get the navy on a war footing. He asked the Naval War College to prepare battle plans in case of war with Spain. With Roosevelt's edits, the plan aggressively called for a near-simultaneous attack of Spanish rule in Cuba, the Philippines (a group of Spanish-controlled islands in the Pacific), and even in Europe itself.

Roosevelt sent Long a regular stream of letters, reassuring him that everything was fine in the office and urging him to extend his vacation. To a friend, Roosevelt was more blunt. "I am having immense fun running the Navy," he wrote.

Roosevelt was a whirl of activity. He issued reports, streamlined navy activities, filled officer appointments, and resolved a long-running dispute over how to organize officers. He also compiled a book of presidential quotations that supported a navy. Through his intellect and willpower, Roosevelt made the status of the navy one of the most important issues in the country.

As acting secretary, Roosevelt visited a naval shooting exercise off the coast of Virginia. He boarded the navy's newest battleship, USS *Iowa*. Almost 1 mile (1.6 km) away, a target craft made from wood and canvas bobbed in the ocean. While Roosevelt eagerly watched, the ship's massive guns swung into position. They fired, creating a roar that threw several bystanders to the deck and burst open locked steel doors. The target craft was blasted into water-logged wreckage. Roosevelt, watching through binoculars, was "dee-lighted."

He returned to shore in rapture. "Oh Lord! If only the people who are ignorant about our Navy could see those great warships in all their majesty and beauty, and could realize how well they are handled, and how well fitted to uphold the honor of America."

REMEMBER THE *MAINE*!

Roosevelt continued to urge Long to build up the U.S. Navy. Specifically, Roosevelt suggested building six battleships, six cruisers, and seventy-five torpedo boats. He also argued for preparation of nine thousand armor-piercing shells, along with a supply of two million pounds (907,200 kg) of smokeless powder.

Tensions with Spain were growing, and Roosevelt acted as if the nations had already declared war. He sent a twenty-page memo to Long, detailing the careless positioning of several U.S. Navy ships overseas. Roosevelt urged that the navy should concentrate these ships in one spot and fully stock them with coal and ammunition. Roosevelt's energy both amused and irritated Long, but he ultimately responded to some of Roosevelt's suggestions. He concentrated the U.S. fleet at Key West. He sent the battleship *Maine* to Havana, the capital of Cuba, in case riots or other disturbances threatened U.S. citizens there.

On the night of February 15, 1898, a tremendous roar from the harbor blasted the balmy Havana air. An explosion had shattered the forward third of the *Maine*, killing 254 men. The ship sank immediately and settled into the harbor's mud, leaving the upper wreckage and a tattered U.S. flag above the water.

THE USS *MAINE*, BUILT IN 1886 AND LAUNCHED FOR SERVICE IN NOVEMBER 1889, EXPLODED IN THE HARBOR OF HAVANA, CUBA, IN FEBRUARY 1898, SPARKING AN INTERNATIONAL CONFLICT.

NEWSPAPERS SUCH AS THE *NEW YORK JOURNAL (ABOVE)* RACED TO BREAK THE STORY OF THE *MAINE*, DECLARING THAT THE EXPLOSION WAS NO ACCIDENT AND THAT SPAIN HAD LAUNCHED AN ATTACK ON THE UNITED STATES. THE UNITED STATES READIED ITSELF FOR WAR.

After receiving the news, President McKinley paced in his White House bedroom through the early morning hours, repeating endlessly: "The *Maine* blown up! The *Maine* blown up!"

No one knew exactly what had happened to the *Maine*, but the U.S. newspapers claimed to know the culprit: Spain. They printed sensational stories—complete with diagrams—of how the Spaniards had detonated a mine beneath the ship. Roosevelt expressed the attitude of many Americans when he claimed that the sinking was caused by "an act of dirty treachery on the part of the Spaniards."

The pressure for war with Spain became unbearable. Long couldn't sleep. When he took half a day off to seek relief, Roosevelt promptly ordered U.S. ships to stock up on coal and ammunition.

On March 26, more than a month after the *Maine* disaster, a government panel delivered a formal report on the explosion to Congress. The panel concluded that the battleship's forward magazines, where the gunpowder and shells were stored, had somehow ignited. The report included no evidence that Cuba or Spain was responsible, but it did indicate that something external to the ship had caused the explosion.

Fired up by newspaper accounts, Americans were convinced that Spain was guilty. "Remember the *Maine*!" became a regular cry. But McKinley hesitated to declare war, prompting Roosevelt to state with disgust that McKinley had "no more backbone than a chocolate éclair." Congress finally declared war with Spain on April 25.

Theodore Roosevelt had been assistant secretary of the navy for only a year, but in that period, he had accomplished an enormous amount. The navy was ready for war. Within hours of the declaration, U.S. naval officers issued orders to confront the Spanish navy. Roosevelt had no intention of sitting behind a desk during the war. He quickly resigned his post as assistant secretary of the navy and joined a new regiment of cavalry: the Rough Riders.

What Really Happened to the *Maine*?

THE DESTRUCTION OF THE *Maine* remains a mystery in the twenty-first century. However, modern historians and scientists believe it was an accident. An internal fire ignited the forward magazine, which exploded and destroyed the ship. Historians note that tiny fires had happened in other battleships that were similar to the *Maine*. No evidence exists to suggest that anyone deliberately started the fire that caused the explosion.

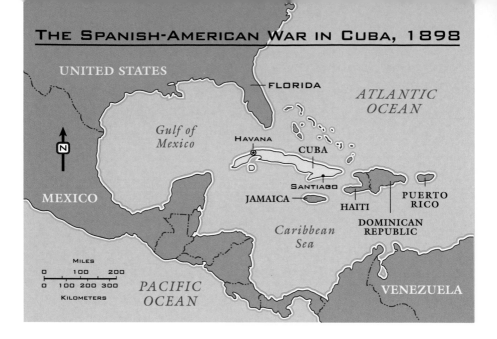

THE SPANISH-AMERICAN WAR IN CUBA, 1898

UNITED STATES

FLORIDA

ATLANTIC OCEAN

Gulf of Mexico

HAVANA

CUBA

SANTIAGO

MEXICO

JAMAICA

HAITI

PUERTO RICO

DOMINICAN REPUBLIC

Caribbean Sea

MILES
0   100   200

0   100   200   300
KILOMETERS

PACIFIC OCEAN

VENEZUELA

THE SPANISH-AMERICAN WAR

On April 25, Admiral George Dewey ordered his four cruisers and two gunboats to leave their position in Hong Kong. The warships left the harbor and headed for the Philippines.

The Spanish fleet, commanded by Admiral Patricio Montojo, was waiting in Manila. Montojo believed his ships weren't strong enough to match U.S. firepower on the open sea. Instead, he moored his ships in a line in Manila Bay, where he hoped the city's guns would help him overwhelm the U.S. ships.

Dewey's force approached Manila soon after nightfall on April 30. Concealed by the darkness, the ships were able to slip past the shore guns and into the harbor. In the growing light of dawn on May 1, Dewey spotted the Spanish fleet.

An officer on USS *Baltimore* later wrote that "the most critical moments of our lives [were] drawing near." Each ship raised U.S. flags

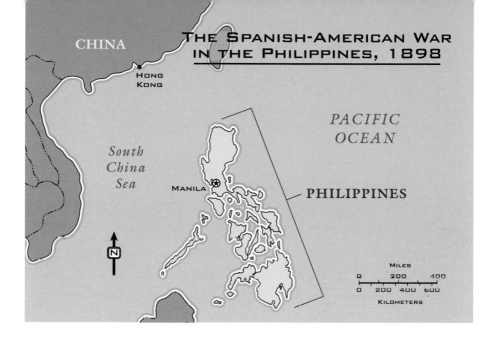

on its masts. "When every man sadly took his station, there was nothing but a grim determination to do or die to be seen written on every face. . . . Those minutes I'll never forget, they seem like hours."

The Spanish ships opened fire, their shells creating geysers of spray and foam around the U.S. fleet. Dewey maneuvered his ships closer and finally told an officer, "You may fire when you are ready." The U.S. guns thundered salvos (a series of shots fired one round after another) at the Spanish line.

Soon, the Spanish ships were in shambles. The U.S. ships for the most part remained untouched. A U.S. observer reported that "the Spaniards fought bravely. But they could not shoot straight."

By twelve thirty in the afternoon, Montojo had surrendered. The Spanish fleet was destroyed, at the cost of hundreds of Spanish lives. In the U.S. fleet, not a single sailor had died. This lopsided victory caused wild celebrations back in the United States, and Dewey became a national hero.

U.S. naval officers searched for remaining Spanish ships in the Atlantic Ocean. Within several weeks, the U.S. Navy had bottled up the remainder of the Spanish fleet in the harbor at Santiago, Cuba. On July 3, six Spanish ships came out of the harbor to fight one last time. As at Manila, the Americans outclassed the Spaniards in gunnery and training. The U.S. fleet poured murderous fire on the Spanish ships, soon battering and sinking them. More than three hundred Spanish sailors died.

The two naval victories, coupled with the success of U.S. ground forces on Cuba (including Roosevelt's Rough Riders), brought the war swiftly to a close. On August 12, 1898—not even six months after the war began—the Spanish signed a peace treaty. Observers in Europe were astonished. "Unless all signs deceive," commented a Scottish newspaper, "the U.S. Republic breaks from her old moorings, and sails out to be a world power."

TEDDY ROOSEVELT *(SECOND FROM LEFT)* AND HIS ROUGH RIDERS HELPED THE UNITED STATES WIN THE SPANISH-AMERICAN WAR (1898).

Speaking Softly but Carrying a Big Stick

While U.S. naval forces had won spectacular victories in what came to be known as the Spanish-American War, Theodore Roosevelt unintentionally upstaged them. At the head of his Rough Riders, Roosevelt had led the attack that broke the Spanish defenses in Cuba. The United States captured Cuba and forced Spain to sue for peace. As part of the peace treaty, the United States took over Spanish territories in the Pacific, including the Philippines. Cuba fell under U.S. protection until it could establish its own government.

William McKinley ran for president again in 1900, with the war hero Theodore Roosevelt as his vice-presidential running mate. McKinley easily won the election but did not serve much of his second term. In September 1901, he was assassinated, and Theodore Roosevelt became president of the United States. When he and his wife, Edith, moved into the White House, she had a huge desk placed in the library. It was carved of timbers from the British warship HMS *Resolute*.

Roosevelt began to seek public support for a large increase in the U.S. fleet and gave a number of speeches promoting the idea. During one speech, he delivered a line that would become famous: "Speak softly and carry a big stick." By this, Roosevelt meant that there was no need to boast or make threats if a nation was well armed. Few in his audience had any doubt that the "big stick" would be a new naval fleet.

The fleet proved necessary, because in 1902 the United States came to the brink of war with a major European power. The trouble began in Venezuela, a country on the northeastern coast of South America. Great Britain and Germany had both loaned the nation large sums of money. When Venezuela couldn't pay its debt, Great Britain and Germany proposed sending a fleet of warships to Venezuela to blockade the coast until the debts were paid.

In Washington, D.C., President Roosevelt reacted with alarm. He did not want to see European power expanded in the Western Hemisphere. Since the creation of the Monroe Doctrine in 1823, the United States had firmly resisted any European expansion in North, Central, and South America. Roosevelt knew that if the Venezuelans didn't repay their debts, the Europeans might seize a Venezuelan port. The port, in turn, would become part of the British or German empire and might house warships that could threaten U.S. interests.

Roosevelt would not allow that to happen. As he settled into his office in the White House, he was confident that he could negotiate with the British. The Germans, however, were different. Germany had become a nation only in the 1870s and was a latecomer to the international stage. Located in the heart of Europe, Germany held enormous power, but many of its leaders also believed that other nations were seeking to thwart its interests. They looked enviously at the French and British empires and eagerly hatched plots in Berlin, their capital city, to build an empire of their own. The German leader—Kaiser Wilhelm II—was known for trying to advance German interests wherever he could.

As the Germans dealt with Venezuela, it appeared that a crisis would be forced with the United States. German naval planners confidently predicted that their warships could defeat the U.S. fleet. In the White House, Roosevelt pondered how to warn off the Germans without provoking war.

As he had stated often, Roosevelt believed that strength would ensure peace. He ordered the U.S. fleet to gather at Puerto Rico, an

Banana Wars

ALTHOUGH THE MONROE DOCTRINE made the Western Hemisphere off-limits to European powers, that hemisphere was not off-limits to the United States. Between the Civil War and the mid-twentieth century, the U.S. Marines landed dozens of times in Latin American countries, including Argentina, Nicaragua, Uruguay, Mexico, Chile, and Panama (then part of Colombia). These interventions typically didn't last long. The marines usually went in to restore governmental or economic stability, or to protect U.S. interests or citizens. These so-called Banana Wars (often fought to protect the interests of U.S. fruit producers) led to publication of the marines' *Small Wars Manual* in 1940. The frequent marine landings in Latin America led many nations to see the United States as a high-handed bully, quick to use armed force to protect its interests.

island in the Caribbean Sea between Florida and Venezuela. Fifty-three U.S. warships, all bristling with guns, came together there. To command the fleet, Roosevelt sent an admiral who was certain to gain notice in Europe. It was Admiral Dewey, famous for his victory against Spain.

On November 12, 1902, the British and Germans announced that they would move against Venezuela to reclaim their debts. This move included sending a fleet of several warships. The Germans had already informed the White House that a "temporary occupation" of Venezuelan ports might be necessary, but Roosevelt believed that an occupation would be anything but temporary. He also knew that the British would not fight the United States over the Monroe Doctrine, because Great Britain wanted to stay on friendly terms with the United States. Germany, however, might take the risk.

Thus Roosevelt spoke clearly when he took the German ambassador aside on December 8, 1902. He told the ambassador that a massive U.S. fleet was near South America. If the Germans seized any territory in Venezuela, the U.S. fleet would intervene and attack the Germans. Unless the Germans settled their claims against Venezuela in an international court, Roosevelt continued, the United States would declare war on Germany. Roosevelt gave the ambassador ten days to respond. After that, the U.S. fleet would intervene.

The ambassador was stunned and confused. Did Roosevelt actually mean to start a war over Venezuela? The ambassador didn't seem to understand that Roosevelt was deadly serious. He merely wrote to Kaiser Wilhelm that anti-German sentiment had risen considerably in the United States.

On December 14, Roosevelt met the ambassador again, seeking a response to the ultimatum. The ambassador didn't have one. Again, Roosevelt stated emphatically that the Germans had to withdraw their threat of force against Venezuela or face war. To make his point clear, Roosevelt declared that he had moved the deadline up twenty-four hours. The Germans had only three days left to make their decision. This time, the ambassador was as frightened as he was confused. In the Caribbean, the U.S. fleet prepared to move.

Only a few people knew that Germany and the United States were on the brink of war. If Roosevelt confronted the Germans openly, the kaiser would not be able to back down without extraordinary humiliation. In short, he would be forced into a corner and would have to fight. Roosevelt had to be extremely delicate. In private, he had told the German ambassador that the U.S. fleet was preparing for war. In public, he said that the fleet was just training in the Caribbean.

The ambassador, however, was still uncertain. He consulted a German friend who knew Roosevelt well. The friend told the ambassador that Roosevelt meant what he had said.

To the newspapers, Roosevelt continued to insist that the U.S. fleet was just training. However, the fleet had begun its cruise to the south. The warships sliced through the water toward Venezuela.

By this time, the ambassador had telegraphed Kaiser Wilhelm, who finally understood the severity of the situation. Just twenty-four hours before Roosevelt's deadline, the German government agreed to resolve their issues with Venezuela peacefully.

Roosevelt's defense of the Monroe Doctrine sent a strong message to the capitals of Europe. During a time when European powers were still carving up the world for their empires, they would not venture again into the Western Hemisphere. The crisis also served as a perfect example of Roosevelt talking softly but carrying a big stick. Roosevelt proved to be a master diplomat in his handling of the kaiser. However, none of Roosevelt's diplomacy would have been possible without the power of the U.S. Navy behind him.

RETURN TO NORTH AFRICA

The crisis with Germany reinforced Roosevelt's belief that a strong navy was essential for preserving peace. Under pressure from Roosevelt, Congress agreed to boost the naval budget by 40 percent, to more than $100 million per year. With this money, the navy built thirty-one new ships—ten of them armored battleships. The United States had the largest fleet in the world after Great Britain's.

Roosevelt soon had an occasion to use the new ships. On the evening of May 18, 1904, a wealthy American named Ion Perdicaris relaxed in his villa in Morocco—one of the four Barbary States. A sudden crash alerted him to intruders. He rushed to the servants' quarters and discovered bandits beating his butler with their rifles.

When Perdicaris tried to stop them, the bandits beat him and tied him securely with cords.

The bandits took Perdicaris out of the house and to their leader, Ahmed ben Mohammed el Raisuli, who headed a gang that opposed the Moroccan sultan, or ruler. Raisuli planned to hold Perdicaris hostage in the remote mountains. He knew the United States would insist that the sultan rescue Perdicaris, a prosperous U.S. citizen.

In exchange for the release of Perdicaris, Raisuli made several demands of the sultan: stop harassing Raisuli's followers, release several of them from prison, pay him seventy thousand Spanish dollars, and give him rule of two of Morocco's richest provinces.

Alerted by Perdicaris's wife, the U.S. representative in Tangier, Morocco, telegraphed Washington, D.C. "Mr. Perdicaris, most prominent U.S. citizen here . . . was carried off last night. . . . I earnestly request that a man-of-war be sent at once . . . situation most serious."

Nearly a century after the United States first fought the Barbary States over abductions of U.S. sailors, Roosevelt confronted another hostage crisis in North Africa. Like Thomas Jefferson, Roosevelt resolved to face the challenge with force. Sixteen U.S. warships were already en route to the Mediterranean on another assignment. Roosevelt immediately ordered several of these ships to detach from the main group and steam to Tangier.

In the meantime, Raisuli reassured Perdicaris that he meant the elderly American no harm. Raisuli explained that once the sultan had met his demands, Perdicaris would go free. But the sultan delivered a message that he would not negotiate for Perdicaris. Raisuli had the sultan's messenger executed.

On May 30, four U.S. warships, gleaming white in the sun, sailed into Tangier Harbor. They fired their guns as a greeting, which drew replies from the Tangier gun batteries. Four marines splashed ashore and went to guard the U.S. consulate. Three more U.S. cruisers arrived the next day.

With U.S. ships crowding his harbor, the sultan changed his attitude toward Perdicaris. But after seven days, the sultan still had not made a deal with Raisuli, and Roosevelt fired off an angry telegraph: "President wishes everything done to secure the release of Perdicaris."

The next day, the sultan agreed to Raisuli's demands. Perdicaris went free on June 24, after a little more than a month as a hostage. When he came down through the mountains, he glimpsed the fleet of ships in Tangier. He then knew it was the U.S. Navy that had applied the necessary pressure to gain his release. "Thank heavens," he wrote "it is that flag, and that people—aye, and that president, behind those frigates," who had given him back his freedom.

THE GREAT WHITE FLEET TOURS THE WORLD

On a pleasant September afternoon in 1906, on Long Island Sound off the coasts of New York and Connecticut, President Roosevelt reviewed the mighty craft of the U.S. Navy sliding by in a line 3 miles (5 km) long. His administration had built most of the ships. "By George!" he exclaimed. "Doesn't the sight of those big warships make one's blood tingle?"

In 1907 Roosevelt had an idea. He proposed that the Atlantic Fleet, including sixteen heavy battleships, embark on a grand voyage from the Atlantic Ocean, around the tip of South America, and into the Pacific Ocean. The more Roosevelt thought about it, the more excited he became. The United States was by then a world power with territories stretching around the globe. What better way to show that it could defend these territories than by sailing a fleet from the Atlantic to the Pacific?

Officially, Roosevelt called the trip a goodwill voyage, but it would prove to be a useful exercise. The U.S. Navy had never conducted such a complicated operation, with so many ships and over such distances. The journey would provide training to sailors and would also demonstrate U.S. naval power. The Japanese appeared to be expanding their empire in the Pacific Ocean, and Roosevelt was determined to block them from taking any U.S. territories there. Roosevelt had also heard that the British and Germans doubted that the United States could keep the big fleet together, repaired, and fueled—and keep its sailors fed—over such great distances. For Roosevelt that doubt was enough reason to try it.

In December 1907, sixteen battleships left Hampton Roads, Virginia, in a line stretching for 7 miles (11 km). The ships were painted white, inspiring Roosevelt to call them the Great White Fleet. Roosevelt was on hand in his yacht *Mayflower*, his face flushed with enthusiasm as the giant ships cruised past. "Did you ever see such a fleet?" he asked onlookers. "Isn't it magnificent? Oughtn't we feel proud?"

The fleet stopped in ports along the coasts of South America, where citizens greeted the sailors with fanfare. As the fleet approached San Francisco, California, Roosevelt revealed his true intention. The fleet would not stop on the west coast but would proceed on a tour around the world—first to Hawaii, Australia, the Philippines, Japan, and China. It would then cruise through the Indian Ocean, the Suez Canal in Egypt, and the Mediterranean Sea before entering the Atlantic Ocean for the final leg of the journey.

The white ships, belching columns of black smoke from coal-fired engines, entered the vast open waters of the Pacific Ocean. The

difficulty of keeping the armada (fleet) together and stocked with food and fuel was enormous. By then the Great White Fleet was a global sensation. Newspapers in several countries—especially the United States—followed its course. Thanks to the fleet's popularity, Roosevelt convinced Congress to pay for four new battleships, as well as the construction of a naval base at Pearl Harbor in Hawaii.

On February 22, 1909, Roosevelt stood on the *Mayflower* and watched with satisfaction as the Great White Fleet steamed back into Hampton Roads. The president had only a few months left in office. In his seven years as president, the U.S. Navy had swelled, from twenty-five thousand men and nine hundred officers to forty-five thousand men and more than one thousand officers. Prior to Roosevelt's presidency, the U.S. Navy had been the sixth-largest fleet in the world. By 1909 it was the second largest.

CHAPTER 6

Covert Operations

TWO BLOODY AND DESTRUCTIVE world wars consumed most of the early twentieth century. World War I began in 1914 when the Allies (led by France, Russia, and Great Britain) fought the Central powers (led by Germany and Austria-Hungary). The United States joined the Allies in 1917. The war lasted until 1918, with the Allies victorious.

Germany after World War I was economically and politically unstable, which led to the rise of the dictator Adolf Hitler. Under Hitler, Germany allied with Italy and Japan and began another world war in 1939. The United States entered this war on December 7, 1941, when Japan bombed the U.S. naval base at Pearl Harbor, Hawaii. The war ended in 1945, and the victorious nations—led by Great Britain, the United States, and the Soviet Union—celebrated.

Both the United States and the Soviet Union emerged as

superpowers after World War II, but there was tension between them. The Soviet Union, centered in modern-day Russia, had a Communist system of government. Those who support Communism believe that capitalism, or free and private enterprise, allows property owners to exploit workers. Communists believe that private property should be abolished. They hold that government should control a nation's economy and distribute goods and services equally among all citizens.

In the years after World War II, the Communist Soviet Union made the capitalist United States and the capitalist nations of Western Europe very nervous. Communism, in the Western view, was just a dictatorship in which a select few individuals seized everything for the state. Under Communism, as practiced in the Soviet Union and other nations, the government ruthlessly crushed people's liberties. The Soviet Union, in this sense, was similar to Germany under Adolf Hitler.

The United States and the Soviet Union regarded each other warily. Thus began the Cold War (1945–1991)—so named because it never became a "hot war" in which U.S. and Soviet soldiers actually fought each other directly. Rather, in a global competition for power and influence, each country sought to support and promote its economic system around the world. That is, the Soviet Union promoted Communism, and the United States promoted capitalism. The Soviet Union set up Communist governments in Eastern Europe and elsewhere. The United States helped nations fight Communist takeovers.

In this conflict, large armies were not the main weapon. Instead, both countries resorted to covert operations. In the mid-twentieth century, few people remembered William Eaton and his exploits in North Africa. But the United States would follow Eaton's example again and again during the Cold War.

Just as James Madison had questioned the use of covert operations, U.S. officials during the Cold War also questioned this tactic. However, they justified it because the danger of Communism seemed so clear. A decorated U.S. Air Force general, James Doolittle, wrote in the 1950s that the United States was facing an "implacable enemy" in the Soviet Union, which sought "world domination by whatever means and at whatever cost."

"Acceptable norms of human conduct do not apply," he continued. "If the United States is to survive, longstanding U.S. concepts of 'fair play' must be reconsidered." Doolittle urged the use of covert operations to "subvert, sabotage, and destroy our enemies by more clever, more sophisticated and more effective methods than those used against us."

Overthrow in Iran

The United States was quick to apply this new philosophy after World War II. One notable covert operation took place in Iran, an Islamic nation in the Middle East. In 1951 the Iranians elected a man named Mohammad Mosaddeq to the office of prime minister. At the time, a number of European businesses operated in Iran. For instance, the British-owned Anglo-Iranian Oil Company pumped oil in Iran and sold it for large profits on the world market.

Mosaddeq pledged to seize British oil production facilities for the Iranian government and free Iran from foreign domination. When he began the process of taking over British oil facilities, the British planned to overthrow him. Mosaddeq learned of the British plot, however, and quickly thwarted it. He expelled British diplomats and shuttered their embassy.

Newly elected Iranian prime minister Mohammad Mosaddeq *(center)* visited New York in October 1951. In May of that year, Mosaddeq angered other countries by announcing that Iran would turn away foreign investors in its oil industry.

Locked out from Iran, the British turned to the Americans. Because Mosaddeq wanted a government takeover of business, the British argued that he was a Communist agent. They said that the Soviet Union, which had occupied parts of Iran in the past, wanted to use Mosaddeq to seize Iran and its valuable oil.

At first, U.S. president Dwight Eisenhower resisted getting involved in Iran. He asked why the United States couldn't "get some of the people in these downtrodden countries to like us instead of hating us." But soon Eisenhower began to see the threat in Iran as real. By then the rivalry between the United States and the Soviet

Union was teetering on the brink of open warfare. U.S. forces were already fighting Soviet-backed Communists in Korea. Eisenhower would consider any moves to counter Soviet influence.

Eisenhower directed Kermit Roosevelt—grandson of Theodore Roosevelt and an officer at the newly formed Central Intelligence Agency (CIA)—to overthrow Mosaddeq. On July 19, 1953, Roosevelt secretly moved into Iran's capital city, Tehran. There, funded with one million dollars, Roosevelt launched Operation Ajax.

First, Roosevelt bribed a group of Iranian news editors, politicians, and mullahs (Islamic religious leaders) to denounce Mosaddeq's rule. He used the same group to call crowds into the streets of Tehran and create an impression of chaos in the city. He hoped that raging mobs, smashing windows and looting, would convince Iranians that the Mosaddeq government was helpless and that the country needed a strong leader. He also hoped to swing the Iranian people around to support the pro-American shah, the nation's weakened king.

Roosevelt met with the shah regularly, sneaking to his palace hidden under a blanket in the backseat of a car. The shah, who had little desire for confrontation or stress, wilted under the pressure. Roosevelt turned to the shah's sister, asking her to buck up her brother's spirits. Again, Roosevelt funded the operation, paying her a bribe that reportedly included a mink coat.

With the shah in agreement, Roosevelt set the coup, or overthrow, in motion. Mosaddeq, however, had heard about Roosevelt's plan. His troops arrested some of Roosevelt's Iranian allies, and at first it appeared that the plan had failed. Panicked by this setback, the shah fled with his wife in a private plane. He finally arrived in Rome, Italy, and told reporters that he did not expect to return to Iran anytime soon.

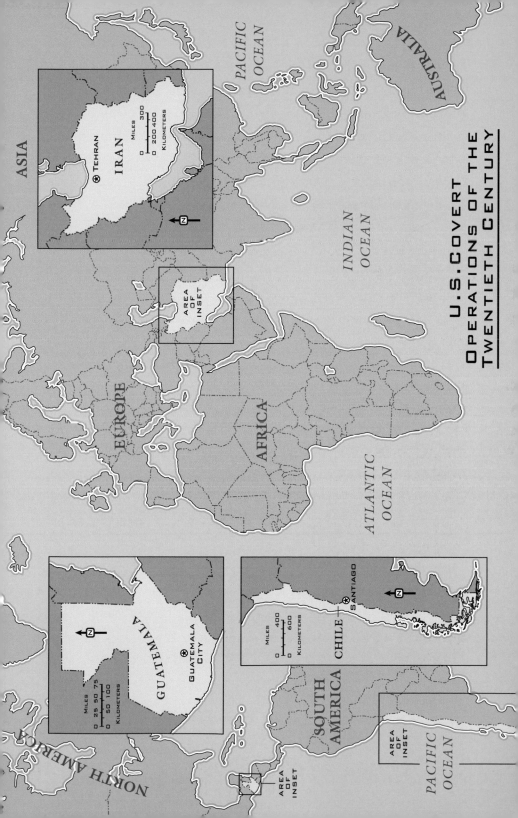

U.S.COVERT
OPERATIONS OF THE
TWENTIETH CENTURY

But Roosevelt had no intention of giving up. Sitting in a bunker beneath the U.S. Embassy in Tehran, he again arranged for mobs to protest against the government. Mosaddeq, believing that the people had a right to assemble and protest freely, did nothing as crowds rampaged through Tehran. The CIA paid many of the protesters, but other groups joined spontaneously, unwittingly supporting Roosevelt's plot.

As part of Roosevelt's plan, the Iranian army entered the streets with guns and tanks. Some of these troops were loyal to General Fazlollah Zahedi, an ally of the United States. On August 19, Zahedi's troops arrested Mosaddeq. Zahedi took over as prime minister of Iran.

The shah returned to Tehran to reclaim his place as king. Roosevelt met him in the palace, where they raised two glasses of vodka and drank a toast. "I owe my throne to God, my people, my army, and to you," said the shah.

In August 1953, Iranian soldiers dampened protests in Tehran, Iran, aimed at denouncing Mosaddeq's government. The United States manipulated both sides of the affair in an effort to reinstate the U.S.-friendly shah.

Riding on tanks and holding images of the shah, supporters of the 1953 coup in Iran celebrate its success.

The aftermath of the coup was multifold. The shah regained power in Iran and proceeded to strip people of their rights and freedoms. He carved up the former Anglo-Iranian Oil Company, keeping 40 percent for himself with the rest going to U.S. and European oil companies.

Many modern historians see the coup as a turning point—at which democracy was crushed in Iran, later resulting in its support of Islamic extremism and terrorism. But in the United States in 1953, government officials saw the coup as a splendid success. The CIA would use covert operations again and again when it confronted governments it believed were threats to U.S. interests.

A Coup in Guatemala

In 1951, the same year Mohammad Mosaddeq took power in Iran, Jacobo Arbenz Guzmán became president of Guatemala, a small country in Central America. At the start of his term, Arbenz announced a bold plan for reform. Like Mosaddeq, Arbenz wanted to break the power of foreign companies in his country, particularly three U.S. companies: Electric Bond and Share, International Railways of Central America, and United Fruit. These three companies, respectively, controlled Guatemala's electrical system, its railroads, and vast tracts of fertile land.

Arbenz announced his intention to build a new power system and construct a new port to undermine the railroad's dominance. Most important, Arbenz sought to wrest land from United Fruit and distribute it among the country's poor.

These reforms gained Arbenz unfavorable attention in Washington, D.C. U.S. leaders charged that he was an agent for the Soviet Union. An investigation of the facts showed that Arbenz had few connections to the Soviets. But the three U.S. companies were angry at Arbenz's plans, and they vowed to remove him from office.

THIS PHOTO OF JACOBO ARBENZ GUZMÁN WAS TAKEN IN 1945, DURING HIS PREDECESSOR'S PRESIDENTIAL INAUGURATION, WHEN GUZMÁN WAS SERVING AS A CAPTAIN IN THE GUATEMALAN ARMY.

They received a sympathetic hearing in Washington, where President Eisenhower was determined to crush any sign of Communism in the Western Hemisphere.

Arbenz first offered United Fruit $1.2 million for 234,000 acres (94,696 hectares) of land. This was the value that United Fruit itself had reported for tax purposes. When it came time to sell the land, however, United Fruit said that $1.2 million was far too low and demanded $19 million. Arbenz refused and had his government seize the land instead. The seizure of private land by the state suggested to many Americans that Arbenz was indeed a Communist and therefore a mortal enemy.

Using Kermit Roosevelt's successful coup in Iran as a blueprint, the Americans planned to overthrow Arbenz in 1954. Allen Dulles, leader of the CIA, budgeted $3 million for the project. In Guatemala, U.S. ambassador John Peurifoy had a six-hour meal and discussion with Arbenz. Peurifoy came away from this meeting convinced that Arbenz was not a Communist but was still determined to use his power against the United States. "It is only a matter of time before the large U.S. interests will be forced out entirely," Peurifoy told Dulles by telegram.

Dulles did not need to hear anything more. He showed Peurifoy's message to President Eisenhower, who found it deeply troubling. The president threw his support behind the plan to unseat Arbenz. The covert operation was dubbed Operation Success, and its budget jumped to $4.5 million.

The CIA needed a Guatemalan to promote as Arbenz's replacement. It picked a former army officer—Carlos Castillo Armas. Armas had already tried to overthrow the government in 1950 and had failed.

The CIA's campaign worked on many levels. While CIA agents helped Armas form an army, Secretary of State John Dulles (brother of CIA head Allen Dulles) isolated Guatemala diplomatically. John Dulles traveled to a meeting of all the countries in the Western Hemisphere. At this meeting, he was able to pass an important resolution, stating that any nation in the hemisphere could intervene if another nation became Communist. These words were vague, but they carried a threat. Everyone knew that the United States would not permit a Communist nation in the Western Hemisphere.

Arbenz was shocked by the resolution. He also knew that the CIA was arming his opponents, such as Armas. Surrounded by enemies, Arbenz tried to buy weapons for his own defense. The United States, however, had blocked other countries from selling him guns or ammunition.

Arbenz then made a serious error: he decided to buy weapons from Czechoslovakia, a Communist nation and a close ally of the Soviet Union. News of the weapons shipment soon reached Washington. To John Dulles, the shipment proved that Arbenz was a Communist allied with the Soviet Union. "That is the problem," he said, "not United Fruit."

The coup was ready. CIA agent Al Haney had recruited about five hundred Guatemalans to serve in a tiny army under Armas. Haney had trained them in camps scattered throughout nearby countries and in Florida. This army gathered in Honduras and on June 18 drove across the Guatemalan border in trucks, with Armas at the head of the convoy.

Haney then unleashed another weapon. Claiming to be broadcasting from a secret radio station somewhere in Guatemala (it was actually in another country), Haney had a steady stream of false information

CARLOS CASTILIO ARMAS *(CENTER)*, LEADER OF THE ANTI-COMMUNIST REBELS AND SUPPORTED BY THE CIA, STANDS OUTSIDE GUATEMALAN REBEL HEADQUARTERS IN JUNE 1954.

and news broadcast to Guatemalans. The "Voice of Liberation" broadcasts sowed confusion throughout Guatemala. Announcers claimed that Armas was making steady progress in his invasion and that Guatemalans were welcoming him.

Arbenz alerted his army and police, who soon whittled down Armas's force. Peurifoy became frantic, believing that Armas needed direct U.S. support. "Bomb repeat Bomb," he telegraphed Washington.

Airplanes roared over Guatemala City, the nation's capital, unleashing gunfire and bombs. The tactic was designed to create confusion and to suggest that Armas commanded an enormous army and air force. In actuality, the fleet was tiny—four fighter-bombers flown by CIA operatives. For the most part, the airplanes made a lot of noise.

Arbenz's situation deteriorated. Guatemalans were confused about the radio broadcasts, which began reporting that the Guatemalan army had deserted Arbenz and joined forces with Armas. Meanwhile, the CIA aircraft continued to attack Guatemala City, terrifying the population.

Arbenz finally agreed to surrender. In a final radio address, he told Guatemalans that "for fifteen days, a cruel war has been waged against us. The United Fruit Company, in collaboration with the governing circles of the United States, is responsible for what is happening to us."

A general, Carlos Enrique Díaz, took power. John Peurifoy was infuriated when he learned this news. The CIA did not want Díaz in power, as he supported many of Arbenz's plans for reform. Furious,

U.S. AMBASSADOR TO GUATEMALA JOHN E. PEURIFOY *(CENTER WITH BOW TIE)* DISCUSSES STRATEGY WITH A U.S. AIR FORCE MAJOR DURING THE GUATEMALAN REVOLUTION IN JULY 1954.

Peurifoy met with Díaz early the next morning. Díaz agreed to resign, but only if the Americans would not place Armas in power. Peurifoy refused and left the embassy in a rage.

"We've been double-crossed," he telegraphed Washington. "BOMB!" A CIA pilot in a fighter-bomber took off from an airstrip in neighboring Nicaragua. The airplane dropped bombs on the central military base in Guatemala City and on a radio station.

After the bombing, Díaz decided to surrender, and yet another general replaced him. This general agreed to meet with Armas, and under Peurifoy's direction, Armas finally took power. Guatemala had a new government and a new ruler. In Washington, D.C., Allen Dulles considered the operation a great victory.

CHILE NEXT

The CIA used its covert operations apparatus as well when another Communist threat emerged in Latin America, this time in the South American nation of Chile. On September 4, 1970, Chileans elected a new president: Salvador Allende Gossens. Like Arbenz in Guatemala, Allende was angry at foreign businesses operating in his country. Foreigners owned most of Chile's vast copper mines, and while the foreign corporations prospered, many Chileans lived in poverty. A self-proclaimed Communist, Allende vowed to seize the mines and reform Chilean society and government.

The CIA was alarmed. It had already spent several million dollars in Chile, paying for the political campaigns of Chilean leaders who opposed Allende. The United States had also helped train Chilean army officers. U.S. leaders saw Allende's victory as a challenge to U.S. power. They also feared that Allende would ally Chile with the Soviet Union.

President Richard Nixon and his national security adviser Henry Kissinger were determined to stop Allende. "I don't see why we need to stand by and watch a country go communist due to the irresponsibility of its own people," said Nixon after the election. Nixon authorized the CIA to create chaos in the Chilean economy and society. If unrest spread through Chile, U.S. leaders believed, the people might turn to an army general to establish law and order.

The CIA used its money to plant articles in Chilean newspapers. These articles described Allende's election in dark tones and predicted that his rule would cause disaster. Anti-Communist groups, also funded by the CIA, staged protests against Allende, and the CIA continued to reach out to Chilean army officers, promising them support if they staged a coup.

The United States also isolated Chile economically. The government pressured U.S. banks to cut Chile off from desperately needed loans, and U.S. companies stopped sending goods and spare parts (for vehicles and other machinery) to the country. Despite this pressure on Chile, Allende had his people's support and was able to take power after his election. For the moment, he had thwarted Nixon, Kissinger, and the CIA. But the operation to unseat Allende continued.

Much of this operation was economic. One U.S. bank canceled a $21 million loan that Chile needed to buy aircraft. U.S. companies refused to do business in Chile. Within a few years, one-fifth of the country's taxis and one-third of its buses were broken down. Mechanics couldn't replace the broken parts because U.S. suppliers wouldn't ship to Chile.

The Power to Wage War

SINCE 1801, WHEN THOMAS Jefferson sent naval ships to confront the Barbary pirates, Americans have debated their president's power to make war. Only Congress has the authority to declare war against another nation, but many presidents have made warlike decisions without congressional approval. One of the most far-reaching instances occurred during the Vietnam War (1957–1975).

Vietnam is a small nation in Southeast Asia. In the 1950s, it was split into Communist North Vietnam and non-Communist South Vietnam. The North Vietnamese wanted to take over South Vietnam and create a single country. The United States was determined to keep South Vietnam from falling to Communists. During the early years of the war, the United States assisted the South Vietnamese with military advisers, weapons, and special units, but did not send combat troops to Vietnam.

In August 1964, U.S. Navy ships were patrolling the Gulf of Tonkin, off the coast of North Vietnam. The ships reported that North Vietnamese torpedo boats had attacked them, and U.S. president Lyndon Johnson used news of this attack to ask Congress for authority to send combat troops to South Vietnam, without a declaration of war. Congress quickly passed the Gulf of Tonkin Resolution to support Johnson's request.

Over the next several years, Johnson sent hundreds of thousands of U.S. troops to Vietnam. When the war turned into a bloody quagmire, with tens of thousands of U.S. soldiers killed, many Americans questioned Congress's action. They wondered why it had given the president such tremendous power to wage war.

In 1973 Congress passed the War Powers Resolution. The resolution requires the president to consult with Congress before sending U.S. troops into harm's way without a declaration of war. Also in 1973, the United States withdrew its troops from Vietnam. Fighting continued until 1975, when the North Vietnamese and their Communist allies in South Vietnam finally defeated the South Vietnamese government.

Communism in Cuba

IN 1959 COMMUNIST LEADER Fidel Castro seized power in Cuba. Castro set up a Communist government—the first such government in the Western Hemisphere—and entered into a close alliance with the Soviet Union. At the height of the Cold War, U.S. leaders were alarmed to have a Communist nation and Soviet ally so nearby.

U.S. leaders were determined to overthrow Castro. The United States landed an invasion force on the island, but Castro crushed it. The CIA devised plots to assassinate Castro, but these failed. The CIA even considered slipping Castro drugs that would cause his beard to fall out. CIA agents suspected that without a beard, the leader would lose his ability to attract attention and thus his grip on power.

Meanwhile, Castro taunted the CIA, stating that Cuba was not Guatemala, where the CIA had easily overthrown the anti-U.S. government. Castro became a symbol of resistance to the United States, which made him a hero to many in Latin America and elsewhere.

The United States was never able to unseat Castro. He remained in office until his retirement in 2007, outlasting ten U.S. presidents. Cuba remains a Communist nation. Castro's brother Raul has taken over as head of the government.

Still, President Allende moved ahead with his plans. His government took over mining operations and the telephone network from U.S. companies. But Chileans weren't satisfied with Allende's rule. Many supporters had expected Allende to transform Chilean society quickly. When that didn't happen, people became restless, which led to demonstrations and violence. Strikes and shortages of all kind rocked the country.

By 1973 the CIA believed that Chileans were ready for a general to restore order. General Augusto Pinochet became the

CHILEAN PRESIDENT SALVADOR ALLENDE *(RIGHT)* POSES WITH HIS NEWLY APPOINTED HEAD OF THE ARMY, AUGUSTO PINOCHET *(LEFT)*, IN AUGUST 1973. IN LESS THAN A MONTH, PINOCHET WOULD SEIZE CONTROL OF THE COUNTRY WITH HELP FROM THE CIA.

nation's top military leader in August of that year. The CIA saw Pinochet as an ally and authorized $1 million to help him overthrow Allende.

On September 11, Pinochet's soldiers seized Chilean radio stations and military installations. Allende and twenty-three of his supporters took refuge in the presidential palace, La Moneda. They armed themselves with rifles, machine guns, and bazookas. By then Pinochet's troops had seized control of the country. Army units began

IN SEPTEMBER 1973, ARMED CHILEAN TROOPS WATCHED FROM A
ROOFTOP IN SANTIAGO, CHILE, AS A FIRE RAGED THROUGH THE
PRESIDENTIAL PALACE DURING THE COUP.

surrounding the palace, and by midafternoon, the palace was aflame.
Then infantry stormed the building. No one is certain what happened
next—whether Allende tried to surrender or not. In any case, the fight
was soon over. Salvador Allende was dead, and Augusto Pinochet was
the country's new leader.

NEW WORLD ORDER

The Cold War continued into the 1980s. During the two-term presidency of Ronald Reagan, the U.S. government sent arms and weapons

to fight Soviet-backed forces in the Central American nations of Nicaragua and El Salvador.

Then, in 1991, the Cold War came to an end. The Soviet economy collapsed, and the fifteen Soviet republics separated and declared their independence. After decades of war threats, the rivalry between the United States and the Soviet Union ended peacefully. The United States appeared to be the last superpower standing, and U.S. leaders spoke grandly of a new world order.

Return to Tripoli

MORE THAN 180 YEARS after the Barbary Wars, in 1986, the United States attacked Tripoli again. By then Tripoli had become the nation of Libya. Libya's leader, Muammar al-Qaddafi, supported Islamic terrorists, and Libyan operatives were linked to several terror attacks, including a bombing in West Berlin, Germany, that killed one U.S. soldier and wounded forty-one others.

To punish Libya, on April 15, 1986, U.S. warplanes took off from Great Britain and bombed several Libyan sites. Afterward, Libya scaled back its terrorist activities—but only briefly. In 1988 a U.S. passenger airliner blew up over Scotland, killing everyone on board. Again, Libyan agents were responsible for the bombing.

Relations between the United States and Libya remained strained throughout the 1990s. In the early 2000s, al-Qaddafi tried to get on better terms with the United States by dismantling his nation's chemical and nuclear weapons programs. In 2006 the United States removed Libya from its list of nations that support terrorism.

CHAPTER 7

The War on Terror

I N THE 1990S, in the aftermath of the dissolution of the Soviet Union, the United States turned to new threats and world trouble spots. The first focus was Iraq, a nation in the Middle East. In 1990 Iraqi armies invaded neighboring Kuwait, a small nation that supplied large amounts of oil to the West. Western nations worried about the safety of their oil supplies and also worried that Iraq would invade nearby Saudi Arabia, another key oil supplier.

In a conflict called the Persian Gulf War (1991), a coalition led by the United States drove the Iraqi army out of Kuwait. Iraqi president Saddam Hussein signed a peace treaty that ended the Gulf War. To maintain the agreement, U.S. troops remained in Saudi Arabia.

The presence of U.S. troops in Saudi Arabia infuriated a Saudi man named Osama bin Laden. The son of a wealthy family, bin Laden had earlier led a group of Islamist fighters against Soviet troops in

Afghanistan. He had founded a group called al-Qaeda to fight the enemies of Islam. After the Persian Gulf War, bin Laden and his followers turned their attention to fighting the United States.

Bin Laden would cite many reasons for his hatred of the United States. Particularly galling to bin Laden were the U.S. troops posted in Saudi Arabia. Bin Laden saw these troops as an extension of the crusaders—Christian, European soldiers who had attacked Muslim lands during the Middle Ages (400s–1400s). Bin Laden also despised the Jewish State of Israel, an ally of the United States located in the heart of the Middle East. Bin Laden believed that Christians and Jews were waging a war to destroy Islam.

Buildup

Islamic hatred for the United States and Israel was not new. As early as the 1960s, some Muslims had formed radical terrorist organizations that attacked U.S. and Israeli targets in the Middle East and elsewhere. In the 1990s, however, the attacks became more and more destructive.

In December 1992, Islamist terrorists bombed hotels that housed U.S. Marines in Yemen, a country near Saudi Arabia. On February 26, 1993, an Islamist bomb expert rented a truck and filled it with the explosive mixture of ammonium nitrate and fuel oil. He parked the truck in a garage beneath one of the twin towers of the World Trade Center in New York City. He lit four 20-foot-long (6 m) fuses and then hurried to a nearby street to watch the explosion. He hoped one tower would fall into the other and kill 250,000 people inside the towers.

The damage was not as extensive as he had hoped, although the explosion did blow through six stories of concrete and steel, killing

IN 1993 THE BLAST FROM A TERRORIST BOMB BLEW A GAPING HOLE
IN AN UNDERGROUND GARAGE OF THE WORLD TRADE CENTER IN
NEW YORK CITY.

six and wounding more than one thousand. The towers shook but
remained standing.

Osama bin Laden wasn't directly involved in these attacks, but
in the late 1990s, he publicly declared war on the United States no
fewer than five times. At first, U.S. leaders dismissed bin Laden as a
crank, but in 1998, he became a genuine threat. That year bin Laden
directed the bombing of U.S. embassies in the African nations of
Tanzania and Kenya. More than 213 people, including 12 Americans,
were killed in Kenya. In Tanzania the bombing killed 11 Africans.

The strikes in Africa demanded a response, and the United
States fired sixty-six cruise missiles at al-Qaeda training camps in

Afghanistan. Bin Laden was not hurt in the attacks, and neither were his top officials. The strikes accomplished little except to raise bin Laden's stature in the eyes of other Muslim terrorists.

Bin Laden struck back two years later. On October 12, 2000, two men in a fiberglass fishing boat approached the U.S. destroyer *Cole*, which was docked in the Yemeni port of Aden. The tiny fishing boat, crammed full of explosives, rammed into *Cole* and exploded. The blast punched a 40-foot (12 m) hole in the destroyer's side and overturned cars onshore. It killed more than seventeen U.S. sailors and wounded thirty-nine. *Cole* was crippled but remained afloat.

The U.S. reaction was muted, which exasperated bin Laden. He had hoped to lure the United States into attacking Afghanistan, where he kept his headquarters. Bin Laden believed that Islamist fighters

IN A TERRORIST ATTACK IN 2000, SUICIDE BOMBERS DROVE A BOAT LADEN WITH EXPLOSIVES BESIDE THE USS *COLE*, DOCKED AT ADEN, YEMEN. THE EXPLOSION RIPPED A HOLE IN THE SIDE OF THE DESTROYER, KILLING THE TWO TERRORISTS AND SEVENTEEN U.S. SAILORS.

could then drag the United States into a quagmire that would drain its treasury and destroy its morale. Bin Laden believed that the United States would be a softer, easier target than the Soviet Union, which his fighters had held off in Afghanistan in the 1980s. With that in mind, bin Laden planned a spectacular strike on U.S. soil that would demand a reaction.

9/11

On September 11, 2001, Islamist terrorists hijacked four airliners in the skies over the eastern United States. Two slammed into the twin towers of the World Trade Center in New York City, which burned and then collapsed. The third plane struck the Pentagon, headquarters of the U.S. military outside Washington, D.C. On the fourth airplane, passengers rose up and fought the hijackers. That airplane crashed in a field in Pennsylvania. The combined attacks killed almost three thousand people.

The United States believed that Osama bin Laden and al-Qaeda were responsible for the 9/11 attacks. By then bin Laden was hiding in the mountains of Afghanistan, protected by the Taliban, a radical Islamic group that controlled most of the country.

The Taliban insisted on a strict interpretation of Islam. In Afghanistan, women had to cover their faces and bodies with heavy clothing when they ventured outside. The law required men to wear beards, forbade Western music, and required participation in Islamic prayer. People who broke important laws from the Quran received death sentences. Sometimes they died by stoning or were forced to jump off a high-dive into an empty concrete swimming pool. To Osama bin Laden, who believed in waging a holy war against all non-Muslims—

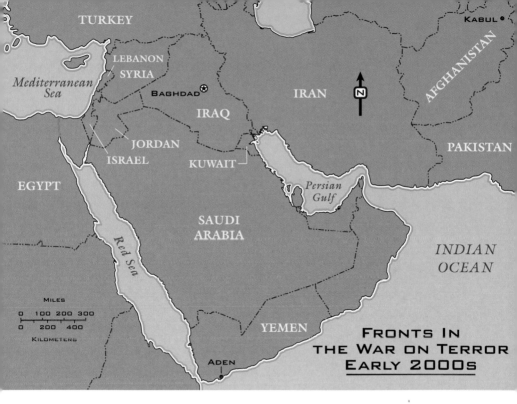

especially Americans—life in the Taliban's Afghanistan was ideal.

President George W. Bush and other U.S. leaders demanded that the Taliban turn over bin Laden. When the Taliban refused, the United States prepared for war. The Bush administration called it the War on Terror.

INTO AFGHANISTAN

Soon after September 11, U.S. special forces teams slipped into Afghanistan. These forces found an ally in Afghani tribes that had long resisted the Taliban, a group called the Northern Alliance, which had battled the Taliban unsuccessfully for several years. In 2001 it occupied only a small portion of northern Afghanistan.

The CIA devised a plan to support the Northern Alliance against the Taliban. The United States would give the alliance supplies, weapons, and ammunition and would also try to buy the loyalty of tribes already allied with the Taliban, paying them to switch sides. Most important, U.S. special forces encamped with the Northern Alliance would direct massive U.S. air strikes against the Taliban's frontline military positions. The CIA believed that the Taliban wouldn't be able to stand up against U.S. firepower.

The airpower would come mostly from the U.S. Navy, which dispatched fleets to cruise the waters of the Persian Gulf and the Indian Ocean. The navy's giant aircraft carriers held hundreds of fighter-bombers. These sleek craft would carry out waves of bombing runs. With precision-guided missiles and bombs directed by special forces on the ground, the navy could project overwhelming firepower over hundreds of miles. President George W. Bush approved the plan.

On October 7—less than a month after the attacks on September 11—the bombing raids began. By then elite special forces from the United States and its ally Great Britain were already working in Afghanistan. Flown in by helicopters from aircraft carriers, these teams carried the sighting devices that would ensure U.S. bombs hit their targets.

The bombing campaign lasted several weeks. To the cheers of Northern Alliance fighters, Taliban positions disappeared under sticks of bombs dropped from giant B-52s. Taliban tanks and armored vehicles supporting frontline troops were targeted and destroyed. Northern Alliance commanders were heartened and impressed. "Today was good," noted one commander after a series of bombings. "The big plane was very good."

With the Taliban weakening, the Northern Alliance began moving forward. On November 9, it captured the key town of Mazar-e-Sharif. The next day, several more Afghani towns fell, and by November 13, the Taliban positions had collapsed. Jubilant Northern Alliance troops captured the Afghani capital city of Kabul. Seven years of Taliban rule in Afghanistan had ended.

In the streets of Kabul, people celebrated. They played recorded music that had been forbidden by the Taliban. Some men skipped the call to prayer and instead went to barbershops for a shave. Women stepped outside without covering their entire bodies.

The fight was not over, however. Taliban and al-Qaeda fighters fled to the mountainous region of Tora Bora in southern Afghanistan. On December 10, 2001, U.S. forces there picked up a radio transmission of a man giving orders. The voice belonged to bin Laden, and he was nearby, but the special forces couldn't find him.

IN 2001 U.S. FORCES IN AFGHANISTAN RODE HORSEBACK ALONGSIDE MEMBERS OF THE NORTHERN ALLIANCE.

In the following weeks, bin Laden disappeared—most likely across the border into the mountains of Pakistan. Although bin Laden remained at large, his power in Afghanistan was broken and his ability to conduct operations against the United States was seriously impaired.

Into Iraq

The United States, in the meantime, had settled on another target—Saddam Hussein of Iraq. President Bush charged that Saddam Hussein, a brutal dictator, was developing chemical, biological, and nuclear weapons (weapons of mass destruction) and cultivating ties with terrorist organizations. In August 2002, the Bush administration described Saddam Hussein as "an imminent security threat that has to be dealt with right away." After months of controversial debate, President Bush ordered U.S. forces to invade Iraq.

On March 20, 2003, U.S. military units invaded Iraq to begin a new campaign, called Operation Iraqi Freedom. Three U.S. Army divisions, one U.S. Marine division, and a British division took part. The columns quickly rolled through the Iraqi defenses, seized crucial bridges, and lunged deep into the country toward the capital city of Baghdad.

As it had been in Afghanistan, U.S. airpower was devastating in Iraq. Three elite Iraqi Republican Guard divisions emerged from Baghdad to confront the offensive. U.S. bombers caught them out in the open and destroyed them. "This affected . . . the morale of the troops," an Iraqi commander later said. "The Iraqi will to fight was broken outside Baghdad."

A sandstorm that one commander described as "a tornado of mud" delayed U.S. forces for several days. However, they soon recovered and began a series of "thunder runs" into the heart of Baghdad. Columns of tanks and armored vehicles made dramatic dashes to the city airport and then into Saddam Hussein's palace. These attacks undermined Iraqi resistance, which soon collapsed.

On April 9, a heavy U.S. truck latched a chain around a 20-foot (6 m) statue of Saddam Hussein in Baghdad and pulled it down. A few weeks later, on May 1, 2003, President Bush boarded the aircraft carrier USS *Abraham Lincoln*. Under a banner reading "Mission Accomplished," he declared the war all but over. The United States then helped Iraq set up a new government that was supposed to operate according to democratic principles.

But troubled voices spoke in the United States. The war had been *too* easy. "The hard part is yet to come," said one retired U.S. commander. "We can easily win the fight but lose the peace." As it turned out, the commander was right. The United States had won its big war in Iraq but ended up embroiled in a vicious small war.

"The hard part is yet to come. We can easily win the fight but lose the peace."
—Colonel Johnny Brooks, referring to the fall of Baghdad in 2003

Within a few months of the "mission accomplished" declaration, U.S. forces in Iraq found themselves facing angry looters, suicide bombers, and entire cities that remained fiercely resistant to both the U.S. occupation and the new U.S.-backed Iraqi government. The country, divided by ethnicities as well as religion, tottered on the brink of civil war.

Conventional Forces versus Terror Tactics

NO MODERN ARMY OR navy would dare challenge the United States to open combat. U.S. forces are too large and too well equipped to lose on a traditional battlefield. So terrorists use another approach in battling the United States and other powerful nations. They use unconventional weapons such as suicide bombers and roadside bombs. Such weapons can be very effective. In Lebanon in 1983, a few suicide bombers were able to destroy a U.S. Marines barracks, killing more than two hundred soldiers. In Afghanistan and Iraq, terrorists fight a shadow war, striking at weak points in U.S. defenses and then melting away into the civilian population when threatened. Such attacks often neutralize the overwhelming U.S. advantage in firepower and technology.

IN JUNE 2008, A U.S. SOLDIER PATROLLED THE SITE OF A CAR BOMBING IN BAGHDAD, IRAQ.

The United States had not destroyed the Iraqi army. Its soldiers had simply melted back into the civilian population. Hiding out in the houses and streets of Baghdad and other cities, they attacked U.S. soldiers with bombings and sniper fire. The attacks grew in intensity day after day, with more and more Americans killed or wounded. Worse, suicide bombers often targeted Iraqi civilians and public places, giving the accurate impression that Iraqi society was disintegrating into violence and disorder.

The insurgents—the forces fighting both the United States and the new Iraqi government—included those loyal to Saddam Hussein, terrorists (including al-Qaeda members), and various factions that hoped to gain power in Iraq after the Americans left. Many ordinary Iraqis, unhappy with the U.S. occupation of their country, supported the insurgents against the United States.

Back in the United States, many Americans had opposed the war in Iraq from the start. They didn't believe that Saddam Hussein had ties to terrorists or possessed weapons of mass destruction—and, in fact, the United States found none there. As the situation in Iraq deteriorated, public opposition to the war grew louder. The public began to doubt a campaign that seemed to be helping no one and had no end in sight.

Hoping to restore order in Iraq, in 2007 the United States began a "surge" against the Iraqi insurgents. Led by General David Petraeus, the surge involved increased U.S. troops and stepped-up efforts to root out insurgents from their strongholds. The surge achieved some success, and as time passed, violence declined.

Even more important than the surge, ordinary Iraqis began to withdraw their support for the insurgents. Most Iraqis regarded the United States as an invader but also believed that the insurgents—

some of them al-Qaeda terrorists—were not necessarily defending the people of Iraq. The Iraqis had witnessed their neighborhoods turned into war zones, with thousands of civilians killed. They, more than anyone, were eager for the fighting to end.

No one knows how the Iraq war and the War on Terror will end. But it is clear that in fighting terrorists and insurgents, the United States is fighting small wars. It is using the same tactics it used during the Barbary Wars. These tactics include small-unit operations, covert operations, and the use of the U.S. Navy to project power. Like the Barbary Wars, the War on Terror will surely offer lessons to future historians and leaders.

The Legacy of the Barbary Wars

THE BARBARY WARS LEFT a long and influential legacy. With these wars, the United States created the U.S. Navy, the U.S. Marines conducted its first operation on foreign soil, and the U.S. government launched its first covert operation in another country. The United States also fought its first small war.

In the aftermath of the Barbary Wars, the United States used small wars repeatedly to protect its interests overseas. The lessons of small wars, first learned on the Barbary Coast, are crucial for modern military commanders.

LEARNING FROM SMALL WARS

Large wars occur on battlefields, as opposing militaries fight one another with similar weapons. The army that most frequently wins on the battlefield usually wins the war. Small wars, however, are typically fought by small, irregular forces. The forces may use unconventional tactics such as suicide bombings, ambushes, and sniper fire to do damage and also create chaos. The traditional battlefield rules do not apply.

In modern small wars, such as the War on Terror, insurgents and other combatants often fight among the civilian population. Fighters do not dress in military uniforms. They sometimes live with civilians, making it hard for more traditional forces to know whom to fight. In such situations, civilian support is key to victory. When insurgents and terrorists can no longer find support among the civilian population, they often lose their ability to fight.

Modern commanders have learned that force is only part of the key to winning a small war. In Iraq, for instance, it isn't enough to blast military installations with airpower. U.S. soldiers also have to restore order in Baghdad and other cities, restore city services, and win the trust of civilian populations. As measures of progress, peaceful neighborhoods, functioning electricity, and rebuilt schools are just as important as the advance of troops. In this regard, small wars require endurance and patience. During the Barbary Wars, the United States had to endure a series of frustrations and setbacks—even humiliation—before securing victory. The same is true in the War on Terror.

COVERT OPERATIONS: THE PROPER USE OF POWER?

The Barbary Wars and other small wars raise many questions. Most important: are covert operations justified to win victory? Many Americans say no. Many Americans were horrified at their government's actions in the Cold War, when the CIA used covert operations to over-throw democratically elected governments in Latin America. After the U.S.-backed coup in Chile, the *Washington Post* asked in an editorial, "How can it be so—if it is so—that in 1970 an American President could consider the possibility of acting to prevent a democratically elected president of a supposedly friendly country from taking office?"

Because covert operations are usually underhanded, sneaky, and devious, the U.S. government often denies their existence. As history writer Richard Zacks put it, covert operations by their very nature "are regarded . . . as un-American." Ironically, many U.S. covert operations were the work of men, such as William Eaton, who considered themselves great patriots.

The United States has changed a lot since Eaton's day. When the nation was young and relatively weak, more powerful countries—especially Great Britain and France—were able to bully it. Even the small Barbary States found it easy to push around the United States. U.S. foreign policy at the time reflected this weakness. The United States had to make some unfavorable peace treaties, as it did with Algiers. In this political climate, the United States felt justified in using any effective tactics, including covert operations, to achieve its goals.

During the Cold War, the United States still felt justified in using covert operations. Many U.S. leaders viewed Communism as a mortal foe. They were utterly convinced that the Soviet Union was preparing a surprise attack on the United States and directing operations to spread Communism around the world.

The U.S. leaders had great resolve in part because they had witnessed the rise of Adolf Hitler in Germany during the 1930s—and the destruction wrought by Hitler's armies in World War II. They were convinced that Hitler could have been stopped earlier, if only someone

IN 1933 THOUSANDS OF GERMANS ATTENDED A NAZI RALLY. THE
NAZIS, LED BY ADOLF HITLER, CONDUCTED MASS GENOCIDE OF
JEWS AND OTHER MINORITIES IN THE YEARS LEADING UP TO AND
DURING WORLD WAR II.

had had the strength and wisdom to do so. They were determined
to stop dictatorships, particularly Communist dictatorships, wherever
possible.

This attitude was idealistic. Indeed, like William Eaton in the
1800s, many Cold War–era leaders spoke about the ideals of freedom
and democracy. But the United States held so much power that it
could also be ruthless in pursuing those ideals.

In addition, journalists and historians have pointed out that many
U.S. covert operations have not led to democracy or freedom. In
fact, they have led to governments that have brutally repressed their

own people, such as the government of the shah in Iran and that of Augusto Pinochet in Chile. The U.S. role in bringing such governments to power has led to worldwide resentment and backlash against the United States.

Journalist Stephen Kinzer, in his book *Overthrow*, argues that the Communist threat during the Cold War wasn't as grave as Americans feared. Most of the leaders the CIA undermined in the 1950s were not Communists allied with the Soviet Union. Instead, they were nationalists—individuals who wanted their countries to have more power over their own resources and less influence from foreigners.

Kinzer argues that the U.S. use of covert operations to overthrow governments has crippled some nations. He points out that Guatemala in the twenty-first century is one of the poorest nations in the Western Hemisphere. Iranian society has experienced repression and unrest since the U.S.-backed overthrow of Mohammad Mosaddeq in 1953. As Kinzer sums up: "Most of these adventures [covert operations] have brought . . . the nations whose histories [the United States] sought to change, far more pain than liberation."

Supporters of the operations charge that they were necessary, if sometimes regrettable, actions in a much larger war against Communism. They believe that Communist nations were a mortal threat that actively sought to spread tyranny around the world, often using covert operations themselves. The coups, supporters say, were necessary to defend freedom.

Unanswered Questions

Other important questions raised by the Barbary Wars involve the importance of defense and the role of the military in the United

States. Few modern Americans would argue that the United States does not need military forces—a navy, a marine corps, and an army. However, the questions Americans first raised about the military two centuries ago still apply. How large should our navy and army be? What is the role of the military in U.S. society? Could the money we spend on the military be better spent on other things? Each generation of Americans must debate and answer these questions.

A lot has changed since 1803, but a lot remains the same. As the United States faces new threats and challenges, it is still using small wars to protect its interests around the world. How Americans conduct these operations—no matter how small—will have an enormous impact on world history.

Modern-Day Pirates

THE WORD *PIRATES* CONJURES images of peg-legged sea captains and swashbuckling fighters of old, but pirates are alive and at work in the modern world. In the Indian Ocean, off the coast of East Africa, pirates from the nation of Somalia sometimes hijack merchant ships and hold the crews for ransom.

In September 2008, pirates seized a Ukrainian ship, *Faina*, along with its twenty crew members and a cargo of weapons and ammunition. The pirates demanded millions of dollars from the ship's owners to release the captured ship. Meanwhile, the United States dispatched warships to keep the pirates pinned against the Somali coast. As of November 2008, the crisis had not been resolved.

The capture of the *Faina* was just one of more than twenty-five hijackings by Somalian pirates in 2008. Just as it did when confronted by Barbary pirates more than two hundred years ago, the international community must figure out whether to pay, fight, or use another tactic to end the piracy.

Timeline

1783	The United States wins independence from Great Britain.
1784	Algerine pirates capture the U.S. schooner *Maria*.
October–November 1793	Algerine pirates seize eleven U.S. merchant ships, capturing more than one hundred sailors.
March 27, 1794	The U.S. Navy is born when President George Washington authorizes the construction of six frigates.
September 5, 1795	The United States signs a treaty with Algiers, agreeing to pay tribute in exchange for the release of U.S. prisoners.
1798	President John Adams sends William Eaton to Tunis as U.S. ambassador.
May 14, 1801	Yusuf Qaramanli, pasha of Tripoli, declares war on the United States.
June 2, 1801	A U.S. fleet leaves Virginia with orders to blockade Tripoli.
July 1801	*Enterprise* defeats the pirate ship *Tripoli* in a sea battle.
May 1803	Edward Preble takes command of the U.S. Navy in the Mediterranean Sea.
October 31, 1803	*Philadelphia* runs aground outside Tripoli. Pirates capture the ship and its crew.
February 16, 1804	Stephen Decatur leads a raid to burn the *Philadelphia* so that it can't be used as a pirate ship.
March 4, 1805	William Eaton and Ahmad Qaramanli begin their expedition across the North African desert.

April 27, 1805	Eaton's forces capture the city of Darnah.
June 3, 1805	The United States and Tripoli make a peace treaty. Tripoli frees its U.S. hostages.
June 12, 1805	William Eaton and Ahmad Qaramanli abandon Darnah.
1812–1815	The United States and Great Britain fight the War of 1812.
October 1813	Captain David Porter lands in the Marquesas Islands and fights a small war with the islanders.
May 1815	Stephen Decatur leads a fleet to the Mediterranean Sea and forces the Barbary States to agree to peace and to pay compensation for the loss of U.S. ships.
December 2, 1823	President James Monroe issues the Monroe Doctrine. It states that any European colonization in the Western Hemisphere will be regarded as a hostile act.
1832	U.S. Marines and sailors storm ashore on the island of Sumatra to confront pirates.
1838	U.S. Marines and sailors again attack Sumatra in response to piracy against U.S. merchant ships.
1853	Commodore Matthew Perry forces Japan to open its doors to U.S. trade.
May 1871	U.S. troops land in Korea but fail to open the country to international trade.
1882	Theodore Roosevelt's *Naval War of 1812* is published.
1897	Theodore Roosevelt becomes assistant secretary of the navy.
February 15, 1898	The *Maine* blows up in the Havana harbor.
April 25, 1898	The United States declares war against Spain.

August 12, 1898	Spain and the United States sign a peace treaty. The United States takes over several Spanish possessions, including the Philippines.
September 1901	President William McKinley is assassinated. Theodore Roosevelt becomes president of the United States.
November– December 1902	The United States and Germany come to the brink of war over German actions in Venezuela.
May 1904	U.S. warships sail to Morocco to ensure the release of a U.S. captive there.
December 1907	The Great White Fleet embarks on a journey around the world.
1939	World War II begins in Europe.
1941	The United States enters World War II.
1945	World War II ends. The Cold War between the United States and the Soviet Union begins.
1951	Mohammad Mosaddeq becomes prime minister of Iran. Jacobo Arbenz becomes president of Guatemala.
July 1953	The Central Intelligence Agency (CIA), through a covert operation, overthrows Mohammad Mosaddeq.
June 1954	The CIA, using Iran as a model, overthrows the Arbenz government in Guatemala.
1959	Communist Fidel Castro seizes power in Cuba.
August 7, 1964	Congress passes the Gulf of Tonkin Resolution, allowing President Lyndon Johnson to send combat troops to Vietnam without a declaration of war.
1970	Salvador Allende, a Communist, becomes president of Chile.

1973	In a CIA-backed coup, General Augusto Pinochet takes power in Chile.
1986	The United States bombs sites in Libya (formerly Tripoli) as punishment for terrorist activity.
1990	Iraq invades Kuwait.
1991	The Soviet Union is dissolved, ending the Cold War.
January–April 1991	U.S.-led forces drive the Iraqi army out of Kuwait.
February 26, 1993	Islamic terrorists bomb the World Trade Center in New York City.
August 1998	Osama bin Laden directs the bombing of U.S. embassies in Tanzania and Kenya.
October 12, 2000	Suicide bombers, directed by Osama bin Laden, strike the USS *Cole* in Aden, Yemen.
September 11, 2001	Nineteen al-Qaeda terrorists hijack four passenger airplanes and crash three of them into the World Trade Center and the Pentagon. Almost three thousand people are killed.
October 7, 2001	U.S. forces begin bombing Taliban targets in Afghanistan.
March 20, 2003	U.S.-led forces invade Iraq.
2007	U.S. troops begin a surge to restore order to Iraq.
2008	Modern-day pirates capture a Ukrainian ship off the coast of Somalia.

Glossary

Arabs: Arabic-speaking peoples of the Middle East and North Africa who share a common culture and history

broadside: the coordinated discharge of guns aboard a ship

capitalism: an economic system characterized by private ownership and free competition, with little government regulation

colonize: to take over and send settlers to new territories

Communism: an economic and political system in which the state owns and controls virtually all business, property, and economic activity

convoy: a group of vehicles that travels together, often accompanied by military protection

coup: the violent overthrow of a government by a small group

dictator: a ruler who holds absolute power and often rules oppressively

insurgent: someone who revolts against the established government

Islam: a major world religion dating to the A.D. 600s and founded by the prophet Muhammad. People who practice Islam are called Muslims.

Islamists: people who advocate the reordering of governemnt and society in strict accordance with the laws of Islam

Latin America: all the Americas south of the United States

Muslim: someone who practices the Islamic religion

nationalism: loyalty and devotion to one's own nation, with emphasis on promotion of national culture and interests

occupation: the holding and control of an area by a foreign military force

Quran: the Islamic holy book

special operations forces: small, elite military forces trained for specialized missions, often carried out in secret

terrorism: the use or threat of violence to create fear and alarm, usually to promote a certain movement or cause

tribute: a payment by one nation to another in exchange for peace or protection

Western: European or North American in outlook, culture, or tradition

Who's Who?

Salvador Allende Gossens (1908–1973): Salvador Allende was born in Valparaíso, Chile. Trained as a physician, he became a politician instead. He was elected to Chile's presidency in 1970. Allende supported Communism, which made him an enemy of the United States. The U.S. government, under President Richard Nixon, directed a campaign to overthrow Allende's rule. In 1973 Chilean armed forces, led by General Augusto Pinochet and backed by the United States, overthrew Allende's government, killing Allende.

Jacobo Arbenz Guzmán (1913–1971): Politician Jacobo Arbenz became president of Guatemala in 1951. Arbenz made enemies by pushing for land reform and other changes in Guatemalan society. He wanted to seize property from international companies, especially United Fruit. The CIA charged that Arbenz was allied with the Soviet Union and in 1954 launched a covert operation to unseat him. Under attack from U.S.-backed forces, he resigned on June 27, 1954. Afterward, he lived in exile in Mexico, Uruguay, and Cuba.

William Bainbridge (1774–1833): Born in Princeton, New Jersey, Bainbridge rose to become one of the highest-ranking officers in the U.S. Navy. He commanded *Philadelphia* when it was captured in the Tripoli harbor and was imprisoned along with the other crew members. After his release from captivity, Bainbridge left the navy and captained a merchant ship. During the War of 1812, he took command of the USS *Constitution*. Under his command, the ship fought a brutal battle with the British frigate *Java*. After several hours, *Java* surrendered, giving Bainbridge military glory at last.

Osama bin Laden (1957–): Osama bin Laden, born in Riyadh, Saudi Arabia, led a group of fighters against Soviet forces in Afghanistan in the 1980s. In the late 1980s, he founded al-Qaeda to fight the enemies of Islam. Bin

Laden declared war on the United States several times in the 1990s. He directed terrorist attacks on U.S. embassies in Kenya and Tanzania in 1998 and masterminded the September 11, 2001, terrorist attacks in the United States. After U.S. forces invaded Afghanistan, bin Laden went into hiding, probably in the mountains of Afghanistan or Pakistan.

Stephen Decatur (1779–1820): Born in Maryland, Stephen Decatur became one of the heroes of the young U.S. Navy. He led the expedition to burn *Philadelphia* in the Tripoli harbor and commanded several ships during the War of 1812. After the war ended, he led a U.S. squadron to again confront Barbary Coast rulers. From ships bristling with guns, he sailed to each Barbary nation and demanded a new treaty. In 1820 another naval officer, James Barron, grew angry with Decatur and challenged him to a duel with pistols. Barron shot and killed Decatur in the duel.

George Dewey (1837–1917): George Dewey, born in Montpelier, Vermont, graduated from the U.S. Naval Academy in 1858. He served in the Civil War under the legendary naval officer David Farragut. In 1896 Dewey took command of the U.S. Asiatic Squadron. During the Spanish-American War, Dewey led the U.S. fleet into Manila Bay, where he destroyed the Spanish fleet, with virtually no casualties. After the victory, Dewey became admiral of the navy—a position never held before or since. Under President Theodore Roosevelt's direction, Dewey commanded a fleet of ships that threatened to attack Germany in a conflict concerning Venezuela in 1902.

Allen Dulles (1893–1969): Allen Dulles directed the CIA from 1953 to 1961. He was instrumental in crafting the U.S. response to the Soviet Union in the first decades of the Cold War. A fierce anti-Communist, Dulles approved operations that unseated governments in Iran and Guatemala. He also made several attempts to overturn Fidel Castro in Cuba. Dulles resigned from the CIA after the Bay of Pigs invasion, an operation against Castro that ended in bloody failure.

William Eaton (1764–1811): Eaton, a veteran of the American Revolution, arrived on the Barbary Coast as the U.S. ambassador to Tunis in 1798. He had his greatest moment of glory in Tripoli in 1805, when he led an expedition across the North African desert with Ahmad Qaramanli. The campaign was the first U.S. overseas covert operation, and Eaton's victory at Darnah marked the first time a U.S. flag was raised over foreign soil. Though recognized widely as a hero in the United States, Eaton's star rapidly faded. His fury at Tobias Lear's treaty with Yusuf Qaramanli, along with his political battles with President Thomas Jefferson, damaged his reputation.

Saddam Hussein (1937–2006): Born near Tikrit, Iraq, Saddam Hussein rose to become his nation's president in 1979. He was a brutal dictator who killed thousands of Iraqi people. In 1990 Saddam Hussein's army invaded neighboring Kuwait, leading to the Persian Gulf War. Hussein had strained relations with the United States for the rest of the 1990s and early 2000s. In 2003 the U.S. government charged that he had links to terrorists and was building weapons of mass destruction. When the United States invaded Iraq in March 2003, he went into hiding. U.S. soldiers found him in December 2003. An Iraqi court charged him with the earlier killings of Iraqis. He was found guilty and hanged in 2006.

Thomas Jefferson (1743–1826): The third U.S. president, Thomas Jefferson was born in Goochland, Virginia. He was a leader in the fight for independence from Great Britain and authored the Declaration of Independence in 1776. Jefferson became the nation's first secretary of state and served two terms as president. During his presidency, he confronted the Barbary pirates and purchased the Louisiana Territory from France, greatly expanding the United States. Upon leaving the presidency, he retired to Monticello, his estate outside Charlottesville, Virginia. From there, he helped found the University of Virginia at Charlottesville.

Tobias Lear (1762–1816): Born in Portsmouth, New Hampshire, Lear was a secretary to President George Washington. President Thomas Jefferson appointed him U.S. representative to Algiers in 1803. After negotiating a treaty with Yusuf Qaramanli for the release of the *Philadelphia* prisoners, Lear was accused of having sold out U.S. interests. He remained in Algiers until 1812. In 1816, for no known reason, he committed suicide.

Mohammad Mosaddeq (1882–1967): Iranian politician Mohammad Mosaddeq became prime minister of Iran in 1951. He was determined to rid Iran of foreign influence, especially British control of the nation's oil and gas facilities. Upset by Mosaddeq's policies, the United States arranged a coup that removed him from office in 1953. The shah of Iran had Mosaddeq imprisoned for three years. After his release, he lived under house arrest until his death.

Ahmad Qaramanli (?–1811): Ahmad Qaramanli was the weaker older brother of Yusuf Qaramanli. Ahmad was in line to assume the throne in Tripoli but was unseated by Yusuf. Ahmad went into exile in Tunis, from where he made several failed efforts to reclaim his rightful spot as ruler of Tripoli. He allied himself with American William Eaton in an effort to recapture the throne. The two men led an army across the North African desert to the city of Darnah. When Eaton was ordered to pull out, he took Ahmad with him. Afterward, Ahmad lived in Sicily, an island in the Mediterranean Sea. Yusuf let him govern Darnah for a few years but then again threatened to kill him. Ahmad fled to Egypt, where he died in 1811.

Yusuf Qaramanli (1766–1838): Qaramanli, the third son of the ruler of Tripoli, was born in 1766. He murdered one brother and conducted an on-again, off-again war with the other (Ahmad) for control of Tripoli's throne. He declared war on the United States when he believed that the other Barbary States were receiving more U.S. tribute than he was. After William Eaton's army captured Darnah, Yusuf agreed to a peace treaty with the United States. He remained on the throne of Tripoli until 1832, when his son took over as pasha.

Kermit Roosevelt (1916–2000): The grandson of Theodore Roosevelt, Kermit Roosevelt was born in Buenos Aires, Argentina. During World War II, he worked for the Office of Strategic Services, a secret intelligence-gathering agency. In 1950 Roosevelt joined the CIA. He masterminded the overthrow of Mohammad Mosaddeq in 1953. Roosevelt left the CIA in 1958 and went to work for oil companies and other firms doing business in the Middle East.

Theodore Roosevelt (1858–1919): Theodore (Teddy) Roosevelt was born in New York City. He held city, state, and federal offices before becoming assistant secretary of the navy in 1897. In this position, he prepared the navy for war with Spain. When war came, he led a cavalry regiment on Cuba and returned to the United States a war hero. He became governor of New York and then joined William McKinley's administration as vice president. When McKinley was assassinated in September 1901, Roosevelt became president. At the age of forty-two, he was the youngest president in U.S. history. Roosevelt served out McKinley's term and was elected on his own in 1904. He passed conservation laws, fought to regulate big corporations, and spearheaded construction of the Panama Canal between the Atlantic and Pacific oceans.

Source Notes

5   Ian Toll, *Six Frigates: The Epic History of the Founding of the U.S. Navy* (New York: W. W. Norton and Company, 2006), 35.

5   Ibid.

5   Ibid., 36.

6   Ibid.

6   Ibid., 41.

10–11   Ibid., 20.

13   Joseph Ellis, *U.S. Sphinx: The Character of Thomas Jefferson* (New York: Vintage, 1997), 75.

13   Ibid., 76.

16   Toll, *Six Frigates*, 33.

16   Ibid., 42.

16   Ibid., 33.

16–17   Stephen Howarth, *To Shining Sea: A History of the United States Navy 1775–1991* (New York: Random House, 1991), 51.

17   Ibid.

17   Ibid., 55.

23–24   Samuel Edwards, *Barbary General: The Life of William Eaton* (Englewood Cliffs, NJ, Prentice-Hall, 1968), 44.

24   A. B. C. Whipple, *To the Shores of Tripoli: The Birth of the U.S. Navy and Marines* (New York: Morrow, 1991), 55.

26 Ellis, *U.S. Sphinx*, 203.

32 Richard Zacks, *Pirate Coast* (New York: Hyperion Books, 2005), 38.

32 Ibid., 39.

33 Edwards, *Barbary General*, 73.

33 Ibid.

34 Whipple, *Shores of Tripoli*, 184.

36–37 Toll, *Six Frigates*, 209.

37 Zacks, *Pirate Coast*, 80.

38 Toll, *Six Frigates*, 211.

38 Zachs, *Pirate Coast*, 41

39 Ibid., 184.

41 Whipple, *Shores of Tripoli*, 187.

43 Zacks, *Pirate Coast*, 174.

44 Whipple, *Shores of Tripoli*, 198.

50 Ibid., 221.

50 Ibid., 222.

51 Ibid.

52 Zacks, *Pirate Coast*, 229.

55 Whipple, *Shores of Tripoli*, 252.

56 Ibid., 292.

57 Ibid., 322.

57   Ibid., 328.

57   Ibid., 304.

60   Max Boot, *The Savage Wars of Peace: Small Wars and the Rise of American Power* (New York: Basic Books, 2002), 13.

62   Ibid., 35.

63   Ibid., 36.

69   Howarth, *To Shining Sea*, 216–217.

72   Edmund Morris, *The Rise of Theodore Roosevelt* (New York: Modern Library, 2001), 588.

72   Ibid.

73   Ibid., 123.

74   Ibid., 590.

76   Ibid., 595.

76   Ibid., 594.

76   Ibid., 595.

77   Ibid.

77   Ibid., 606.

78   Ibid., 610.

80   Ibid., 626.

80   Ibid., 627.

81   Ibid., 638.

82–83   Howarth, *To Shining Sea*, 255.

83 Ibid., 257.

84 Ibid., 271.

 5 Toll, *Six Frigates*, 466.

90 Edmund Morris, *Theodore Rex* (New York: Modern Library, 2002), 324.

91 Ibid., 329.

91 Ibid., 338.

91 Ibid., 455.

92 Ibid., 467.

96 Ibid., 198–199.

97 Ibid., 122.

100 Stephen Kinzer, *Overthrow: America's Century of Regime Change from Hawaii to Iraq* (New York: Times Books, 2006), 128.

103 Ibid, 137.

104 Ibid., 140.

105 Tim Weiner, *Legacy of Ashes: The History of the CIA* (New York: Anchor, 2008), 145.

106 Kinzer, *Overthrow*, 145.

107 Ibid., 146.

108 Ibid., 180.

120 David Rhode, "Sight of a B-52 Makes Northern Alliance Troops Shout with Joy," *New York Times*, November 1, 2001, http://query.nytimes.com/gst/fullpage.html?res=9A06E6DF1030F932A35752C1A9679C8B63 (September 26, 2008).

122 Thomas E. Ricks, *Fiasco: The U.S. Military Adventure in Iraq* (New York: Penguin Press, 2006), 46.

122 Ibid., 125.

122 Ibid.

123 Ibid., 134.

123 Ibid.

129 Ibid., 188.

129 Zacks, *Pirate Coast,* 43.

131 Kinzer, *Overthrow*, 322.

Selected Bibliography

Atkinson, Rick. *In the Company of Soldiers: A Chronicle of Combat.* New York: Henry Holt and Company, 2004.

Boot, Max. *The Savage Wars of Peace: Small Wars and the Rise of American Power.* New York: Basic Books, 2002.

Edwards, Samuel. *Barbary General: The Life of William Eaton.* Englewood Cliffs, NJ: Prentice-Hall, 1968.

Ellis, Joseph. *U.S. Sphinx: The Character of Thomas Jefferson.* New York: Vintage, 1997.

Howarth, Stephen. *To Shining Sea: A History of the United States Navy 1775–1991.* New York: Random House, 1991.

Kinzer, Stephen. *All the Shah's Men.* Hoboken, NJ: John Wiley and Sons, 2008.

———. *Overthrow: America's Century of Regime Change from Hawaii to Iraq.* New York: Times Books, 2006.

McCullough, David. *John Adams.* New York: Simon and Schuster, 2001.

Morris, Edmund. *The Rise of Theodore Roosevelt.* New York: Modern Library, 2001.

———. *Theodore Rex.* New York: Modern Library, 2002.

Ricks, Thomas E. *Fiasco: The U.S. Military Adventure in Iraq.* New York: Penguin Press, 2006.

Smith, Michael. *Killer Elite: The Inside Story of America's Most Secret Special Operations Team.* New York: St. Martin's Press, 2006.

Toll, Ian. *Six Frigates: The Epic History of the Founding of the U.S. Navy.* New York: W. W. Norton and Company, 2006.

Weiner, Tim. *Legacy of Ashes: The History of the CIA.* New York: Anchor, 2008.

Whipple, A. B. C. *To the Shores of Tripoli: The Birth of the U.S. Navy and Marines.* New York: Morrow, 1991.

Wright, Lawrence. *The Looming Tower: Al Qaeda and the Road to 9/11.* New York: Alfred A. Knopf, 2006.

Zacks, Richard. *Pirate Coast.* New York: Hyperion Books, 2005.

Further Reading, Films, and Websites

Books

Arnold, James R. *Saddam Hussein's Iraq*. Minneapolis: Twenty-First Century Books, 2009. As president of Iraq, Saddam Hussein ruled as a brutal dictator. This book examines his rise to power, life in Hussein's Iraq, and his eventual capture and execution during the Iraq War.

Behrman, Carol. *Thomas Jefferson*. Minneapolis: Twenty-First Century Books, 2004. A leader in the fight for independence and the third president of the United States, Jefferson led the United States through its first small wars—against the Barbary pirates. This biography examines Jefferson's life, work, and political legacy.

Childress, Diana. *The War of 1812*. Minneapolis: Twenty-First Century Books, 2004. The War of 1812 gave the United States its first test against a major world power—Great Britain. This book chronicles the war, its battles, and the soldiers and leaders on both sides of the fight.

Dolan, Edward F. *The Spanish-American War*. Minneapolis: Twenty-First Century Books, 2001. In 1898 the United States was itching for war with Spain. That war began after the U.S. warship *Maine* blew up in Havana, Cuba. This book looks at the Spanish-American War in great detail—from the ordinary soldiers to the battles to the home front.

Landau, Elaine. *Osama bin Laden: A War against the West*. Minneapolis: Twenty-First Century Books, 2002. Osama bin Laden is a shadowy figure. His whereabouts are a mystery. This book examines what is known—and still unknown—about the mastermind of the 9/11 terrorist attacks.

McPherson, Stephanie Sammartino. *Theodore Roosevelt*. Minneapolis: Twenty-First Century Books, 2005. The United States grew into a world power under the guidance of Theodore Roosevelt, who championed a strong U.S. Navy. As assistant secretary of the navy and president of the United States,

Roosevelt was able to put many of his ideas for U.S. naval power into action. This book tells Roosevelt's life story.

Sherman, Josepha. *The Cold War*. Minneapolis: Twenty-First Century Books, 2007. In the late twentieth century, the United States and the former Soviet Union viewed each other as mortal enemies. The nations didn't fight directly but instead used covert operations and other tactics to promote their interests around the world. The U.S. overthrow of governments in Iran, Guatemala, and Chile were all Cold War campaigns.

Zwier, Lawrence J., and Matthew S. Weltig. *The Persian Gulf and Iraqi Wars*. Minneapolis: Twenty-First Century Books, 2005. The United States has gone to war in Iraq twice—once in 1991 and again in the early twenty-first century. This book explores the reasons for war, the troops and equipment, and the major battles and turning points.

Films

Battle History of the Navy. DVD. New York: A&E Television Networks, 2000. The U.S. Navy was born when President George Washington authorized the building of six frigates in 1794. This film traces the growth of the navy as a fighting force.

The Battle of Tripoli. DVD. New York: A&E Television Networks, 2004. This straight-forward documentary describes the campaign against Yusuf Qaramanli in Tripoli, including William Eaton's 1805 march through the North African desert.

Spanish-American War: Birth of a Superpower. DVD. New York: A&E Home Video, 2005. This film explores the causes of the Spanish-American War, how it was fought, and how it propelled the United States onto the world stage.

War on Terror. DVD. New York: A&E Home Video, 2007. This video examines the U.S.-led War on Terror and how it is being fought in spots around the globe, especially in the Middle East.

Websites

BBC Special Reports: Investigating Al Qaeda
http://news.bbc.co.uk/2/hi/in_depth/world/2001/war_on_terror/default.stm
This website is rich with accounts of al-Qaeda, the extremist terrorist organization led by Osama bin Laden. Created by the British Broadcasting Corporation, the site explores the group's history and how forces around the world are trying to stop it.

Naval Historical Center
http://www.history.navy.mil/index.html
This website is a treasure trove of information on the U.S. Navy and its history.

Small Wars Center of Excellence
http://www.smallwars.quantico.usmc.mil/
On this website, the U.S. Marine Corps documents how it fights modern small wars.

War against Terror
http://www.cnn.com/SPECIALS/2001/trade.center/
This website from CNN explores the War on Terror, with historical background as well as up-to-date news reports.

Index

Darnah, Tripoli, 40, 42, 51–55
Decatur, Stephen, 36–38, 58–59, 140
Dewey, George, 82–83, 140
Díaz, Carlos Enrique, 106–107
Donaldson, Joseph, 21
Doolittle, James, 96
Downes, Jack, 65–66
Dulles, Allen, 103, 106, 140
Dulles, John, 104

Eaton, William, 95, 141; appointed ambassador to Tunis, 23–26; attack on Darnah, 51–55; betrayed by U.S. negotiations, 54–56; crosses desert to Bomba, 40–51; journal, 49; plans and schemes, 32–34
Eclipse (United States), 66
Eisenhower, Dwight, 97–98
Electric Bond and Share, 102
England. See Great Britain
Enterprise, USS, 27, 28–31
Essex, USS, 27, 60–61
Europe: Algiers-Portuguese treaty, 4; assistance in Barbary War, 41–53; colonialism, expansion, and Monroe Doctrine, 64, 71, 74, 87–89; Communism in Eastern, 95; fights against Barbary States, 59; influence and business in Iran, 96, 101; Jefferson and Adams in, 13; as market for U.S. goods, 12; respect for United States from, 16–17; terrorized by Barbary pirates, 4, 9–10. *See also* Great Britain

Faina (Ukraine), 132
Fillmore, Millard, 67
Franklin, Benjamin, 12
Friendship (United States), 65
frigates, 18

Georgia, 19
Germany, 85–89, 94
Gift of Allah (Tripoli), 35
Great Britain: British navy, 11; colonialism and Monroe Doctrine, 64; combating terrorism, 120; in Iran, 96–97; in Iraq war, 122; naval bombardment of Algiers, 59; trade relations with United States, 11–12; treaties and tribute with Barbary States, 9, 10; Venezuela incident, 85–89; War of 1812, 57–58, 59, 60–63; in World Wars, 94. *See also* Europe
Great White Fleet tour, 91–93
Guatemala, 102–107
Gulf of Tonkin Resolution, 109
Gulf War (Iraq), 114

Hamilton, Alexander, 14
Haney, Al, 104
Happah tribe (Marquesas), 61–63
Hassan Pasha, Dey, 21
Hitler, Adolf, 94, 129–130
Hong Kong, 69
Hornet, USS, 52
Hull, Isaac, 40, 41
Humphreys, Joshua, 18–21
Hussein, Saddam, 122, 125, 141

International Railways of Central America, 102
Intrepid, USS, 36–38
Iowa, USS, 78
Iran, 96–101
Iraq: Iraq war, 122–126; Persian Gulf War, 114
Islam, 8, 13
Islamic extremism, 101, 115–126. *See also* terrorism

Japan, 67–68

About the Author

Brendan January is an award-winning author of more than twenty nonfiction books for young readers. His works include *The Iranian Revolution* and *The Arab Conquests of the Middle East* for the Pivotal Moments in History series. Educated at Haverford College and the Columbia Graduate School of Journalism, January was also a Fulbright Scholar in Germany. He lives with his wife and two children in Maplewood, New Jersey.

Photo Acknowledgments